photographing
Charleston, Savannah
& the Coastal Islands

Where to Find Perfect Shots and How to Take Them

Jeff Dodge

D1605475

THE COUNTRYMAN PRESS
WOODSTOCK, VERMONT

Photographing Charleston, Savannah & the Coastal Islands

ISBN 978-0-88150-921-2

Maps by Paul Woodward, © The Countryman Press
Book design and composition by S. E. Livingston

Published by The Countryman Press,
P.O. Box 748, Woodstock, VT 05091

Distributed by W. W. Norton & Company, Inc.,
500 Fifth Avenue, New York, NY 10110

Printed in the United States of America

10 9 8 7 6 5 4 3 2 1

*Title page: North Adger Wharf off of East
Bay Street, Charleston;* GPS coordinates:
32°46'31" N, 79°55'37" W

*Right: Simple image of a pelican—my favorite
bird—near Frampton Inlet, Botany Bay.*
GPS coordinates: 32°32'16" N, 80°15'30" W

Acknowledgments

You can never go far in life without friends and family, all of whom were invaluable in helping me assemble this book.

My photographer friend Warren Lieb recommended me for this assignment. His dedication to the film and photographic processes and his love of the visual vehicle as a form of transcendence are a constant inspiration, and his editing skills helped tune the contents.

My son, Will, and my daughter, Arden, continually make my soul sing, and I know the love they inspire has had a profound effect on my ability to see.

This book would not have been possible without my wife, Colleen. In addition to running her own communications company, juggling a college teaching position along with the lives of our two school-age children, volunteering on the boards of charitable foundations, and running our household, she found the time to edit the text of this effort and keep me on task throughout. She is my light and my hero. This book is for her.

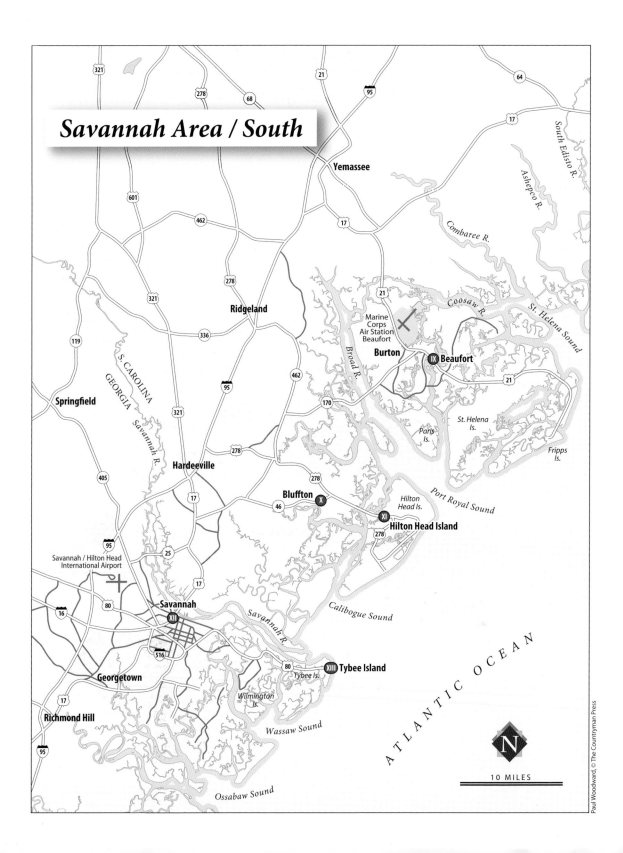

Savannah Area / South

10 MILES

Paul Woodward, © The Countryman Press

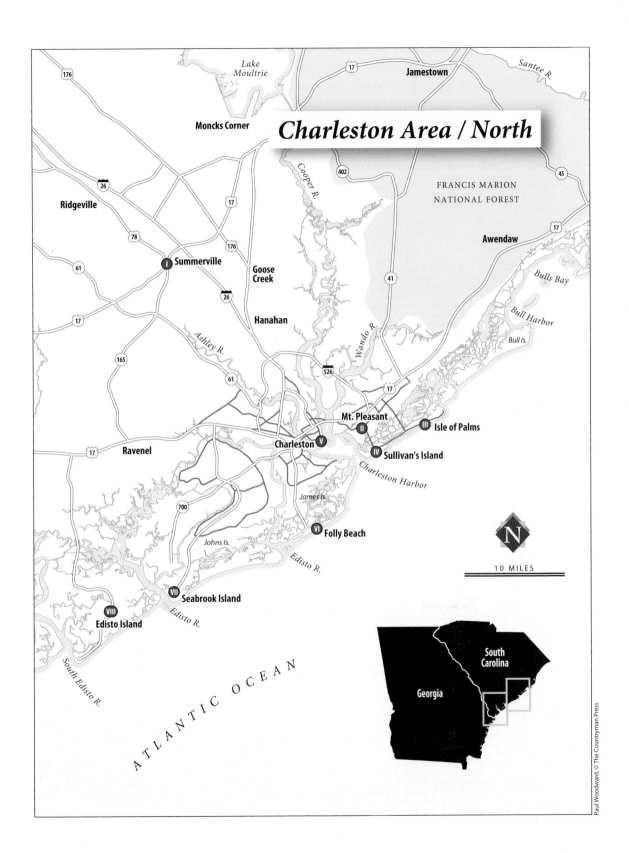

Charleston Area / North

Lake Moultrie

Santee R.

Jamestown

176

17

Moncks Corner

Cooper R.

402

45

FRANCIS MARION
NATIONAL FOREST

26

Ridgeville

17

176

Awendaw

17

78

61

I Summerville

Goose
Creek

41

Bulls Bay

26

Bull Harbor

17

Hanahan

Bull Is.

Ashley R.

Wando R.

165

526

61

17

Mt. Pleasant

II

III Isle of Palms

Ravenel

17

Charleston

V

IV Sullivan's Island

Charleston Harbor

James Is.

700

VI Folly Beach

Johns Is.

Edisto R.

N

10 MILES

VII Seabrook Island

Edisto R.

VIII Edisto Island

South Edisto R.

ATLANTIC OCEAN

South
Carolina

Georgia

Helen's chair, Front Beach, Isle of Palms; GPS coordinates: 32°46'58" N, 79°47'36" W

Contents

Introduction

"You gotta carry a camera. You can't even take a bad picture without one."

Those words were passed along to me from Dan Dry, *National Geographic* photographer and 1981 National Press Photographer of the Year. I met Dan in the early '80s, as my career was starting. He's what photo editors call, "a good shooter," and I longed for a career that would follow his path.

Soon, my aspirations collided with reality. My first job involved bribing a mailman to provide entree to a tenant's mailbox. The tenant's name was on the inside of the mailbox, proving theirs was an illegal sublet. I guarantee you that was the most extensively photographed mailbox in the history of the postal service.

The nadir of my career, you suggest? Sadly, I've done worse. A coffee shop was dumping their garbage in the basement of an office building. The landlord was not pleased and wanted a record of the garbage heap; guess who got the assignment? When the restaurant owner saw me shooting, he physically threatened me and demanded I hand over the film. I, of course, acquiesced.

Ahh, the glorious, glamorous world of the professional photographer!

Time passed, and my career improved. I started shooting products, people, and places. Assignments took me throughout NYC and off to Asia. And I got paid for it. What a world!

Today, I am based in the gorgeous Lowcountry of South Carolina. And I rarely leave home without a camera.

Of course, decorum dictates that when attending a beach wedding, I refrain from grabbing shots as an osprey dive bombs the water, grabs a silvery fish, and flies right over my head.

Travel as if you intend to shoot. The good news is you don't need a lot of equipment. A long lens is required to shoot wildlife, and a heaping helping of patience is requisite. Map-reading skills are helpful, and a fine-tuned sense of when to be where is key. For instance, it is advantageous to know that light falls on the entrance to Charleston's USS *Yorktown* at a certain time in the morning. Aircraft carriers are tough to fill-flash.

Great images don't always just happen. Patience and diligence are rewarded, and it may take more than one trip to a location to snag the perfect image. *National Geographic* photographers are famous for returning to a location many, many times. They keep coming back until they've captured the very best a location has to offer. We are not all so lucky. Most of us pass a place once and move on.

Iconic landmarks are always popular to shoot. The real challenge is to provide a new perspective. Find a novel way to shoot the Eiffel Tower, and you just might get published. If I want to hang a photograph on my wall, I know when I've shot a winner. At the very least, your friends and family will look at your vacation photos willingly!

By default, any "guide" is a how-to. A travel guide will tell you how to get from A to B and what to see along the way. A photography guide will tell you how to grab interesting shots. I have featured locations in this book for their esthetic value and attractiveness as destinations. An expanse of open marsh may hold a beautiful sunset one day and be a gray, dull vista the next. I'm trying to send you where things are reliably interesting.

The book starts in Summerville, South Carolina, and wends its way to Tybee Island, Georgia, south of Savannah.

I have included GPS coordinates from each location so you can reprise a particular shot and apply your special influence. You may enjoy shooting shore birds or landscapes, working folks or door knockers. I strive in this book to offer tips to accommodate various approaches to travel photography.

You won't see ice floes or forests of kaleidoscopic autumnal leaves. But you will see beautiful marshes and pine forests, Spanish moss and lizards, ibis and pelicans and osprey. The flora and fauna of the coastal Carolinas and Georgia are particularly beautiful; the historic and contemporary architecture is unique.

I tried to let the beauty speak for itself. Digital techniques offer those with photo-related software skills the option to markedly alter their original photographs. In this book, we will make only those changes that could be made in a traditional darkroom, including dodging and burning and color enhancement. Otherwise, this would be a book about photo manipulation.

In addition, I will focus on digital photography technologies and only briefly touch on film techniques. Digital means we no longer worry about the types of film we're using.

No matter your skill or experience level, my aim here is to help you get the images that will make you smile long after you've left the Lowcountry behind.

And remember to always pack your camera! Providence and planning will reward you with beautiful memories of your travels.

Architectural detail, East Liberty Street, Savannah; GPS coordinates: 32°4'29" N, 81°5'36" W

Using This Book

This book follows a north to south route, from Summerville, SC, outside of Charleston, SC, to Tybee Island, outside of Savannah, GA. I expect that everyone has his or her own itinerary; travels, like life, do not usually follow a linear path.

I don't assume that I am going to find the single best place to shoot at any locale. I have learned that when I return to a location, something has usually changed from my previous visit. For instance, I can return to Isle of Palms or Sullivan's Island to find a movie being shot, people throwing cast nets from a jetty or rod fishing from the pier. At other times, folks will be flying kites; wind-, kite-, and board surfing; air skateboarding; biking; jogging; dolphin watching; and dog walking. You will come away with images that are undeniably different and undoubtedly more interesting than mine— I just want you to know that you should look around because there might be something of interest to photograph.

This book is not a technical manual that addresses a particular level of photographic competency. I assume that everyone is at a different photographic skill level, so I have tried to offer technical information that will be helpful to most. I think it may be useful to understand why I did what I did in a certain situation. I'm sure that I will appear to be master of the obvious to some while being revelatory to others. When appropriate, I'll let you know how I photographed each location and why I used a particular lens or shot from a particular angle.

When a location is difficult to find, I've tried to leave a trail of breadcrumbs. In addition, I've included GPS location data wherever possible so you can find the location on Google Maps or input that data into your own GPS. GPS data can be found with the caption information for each photograph. This book is as much a guide as it is a series of suggestions. If you think a location might yield a promising photo-op, stop the car or get off the bike, lay down your camera bag, and shoot. Inspirational opportunities are short-lived. Don't let them pass you by.

I encourage you to trust your intuition and explore.

Charleston's Arthur Ravenel Jr. Bridge, familiarly known as the New Cooper River Bridge, was completed in 2005. The bridge's main span is 1,546 feet, the longest cable-stayed bridge in the Western Hemisphere. The bicycle and pedestrian path is a great spot to photograph the USS Yorktown aircraft carrier, cruise ships steaming into port, or the northern coast of the Charleston peninsula. There are plenty of spots from which to shoot the bridge but I think the best perspective can be found at Waterfront Memorial Park, located on the Mount Pleasant side at the base of the bridge. GPS coordinates: 32°48'7" N, 79°54'10" W

A montage of 2-megapixel images from my camera phone.

How I Photograph Charleston, Savannah & the Coastal Islands

My Camera Gear

Some years ago, a photo magazine would feature in every issue a celebrity shooter and show readers the contents of his (or her) camera bag. I found it fascinating and comforting to know that everyone does it pretty much the same way.

You could choose a hard case for a camera bag, such as those made by Pelican or Halliburton. Or you could choose a structured soft case like those made by Tenba and Tamrac. You might prefer a canvas bag with no support, like those made by Domke, a knapsack case to hike or climb with, a camera bag on wheels, or something that looks like a mailbag. (The last was preferred by shooters trying to confuse camera thieves.)

Truth is, it matters little what you carry your camera in, as long as you carry a camera, or two.

For this section, I'll assume you're using a digital SLR (single lens reflex) and that you work with a setting other than Program or Automatic. I'll talk about point-and-shoot cameras later. I've always felt that solid-state electronics should be infallible, but humidity, dust, sand, sea air, and constant knocking around will inevitably lead to camera failure.

I started my career doing public relations and press work in New York. One of my mentors used to rail at me for always carrying such a big camera bag. Meanwhile, he would go on jobs with just one camera, one zoom lens, and one flash. On the inevitable day his camera failed, he asked to borrow one of mine. Of course, I refused (just long enough for apoplexy to set in); but he never again worked with just one camera body. If you're on the job and you can't take a picture, you are up the prover-

bial creek without a paddle. The embarrassment quotient is DEFCON 4. You are also minus one client.

Even if you are shooting purely for pleasure, reliability and accessibility are key. Have your camera, protect it, know that it works, and confidently grab those defining photos.

For photographers at all levels, equipment is the extension of your technical and sensory skills. It's there to enable the capture of a scene. Don't get hung up on having to use the latest greatest; all the originators, like Cartier-Bresson, Brassai, Steiglitz, and their ilk, worked with equipment that today we would consider quaint and comical.

Turn off the motor drive and slow down to examine the light and compose the scene. Work with a tripod. A healthy dose of anticipation is one of the most beneficial pieces of equipment you could acquire. Patience and diligence are also great tools.

And, of course, serendipity plays a starring role in any photographer's arsenal. But serendipity seldom works alone. To be ready for that magical moment, one's equipment must work flawlessly.

Tips:

• Ensure that both front and rear elements of your lens are clean. It only takes 5 minutes for the oil from your skin to permanently adhere to a camera lens. Wipe lenses with a soft cloth (and a warm breath) starting from the center and working your way to the edge in a circular motion. Caution: Blow dust off first! I was once working at an aluminum plant. I didn't realize there were minute particles of aluminum in the

A 300mm lens and 2x tele extender brought this fisherman close while exaggerating the wave action. **GPS coordinates: 32°46'28" N, 79°48'50" W**

air, sharp enough to scratch the lens coating of my new zoom when I tried to clean it. It would have cost more to have the lens recoated than to buy a new one. It's still functional, but I only use it as a knock-around lens; I never use it on important shoots.

• Clean corroded battery contacts, hot shoes, and flash contacts with a pencil eraser—it will clear that blue-green, dried battery acid away in seconds. You can also use an X-Acto blade to scrape off battery acid. Grooving the metal will also assist connectivity.

• Find the best way to clean your camera's sensor. Learn how to lock up the mirror on your SLR and get a good blower like the Rocket Blaster to flush away the dust your electromagnetically charged sensor loves to attract. Some cleaning tools use a sticky adherent to grab dust from your sensor, but I'm from the don't-ever-touch-your-sensor school, because sensors scratch very easily.

Some cameras will shake the sensor thousands of times upon start-up, shutdown, or on command to loosen dust. One black speck of dust on an afternoon's session will lead to hours of postproduction work. And rest assured, that speck will find its way into your gorgeous sunsets and will be smack dab in the middle of people's foreheads, it never lands on the black cat. Be aware that dust can also creep into your lens and potentially cause diffraction issues and affect lens sharpness. You will need to return the lens to the manufacturer or an authorized repair shop to clean out any rogue specks.

People always say to me, "I love this camera, it takes great pictures." The camera itself is the least important piece of your equipment. Sure, you should take the time to diligently review the camera menu and functions. It's a good bet you won't use 85 percent of the camera's capabilities, but it's good to know what it can do. If you're unsure of something, look it up in the camera manual. Mine is always in my bag, and I refer to it constantly. (I have no problem asking for directions when driving, either.)

A good, sharp lens that offers swift focusing is paramount. The optics on zoom lenses have improved, but you will always fare better (sharper) with a fixed focal length lens. It used to be that Nikon and Zeiss offered superior quality lenses, but that playing field has leveled. Nikon, Canon, Olympus, Fuji, Minolta, and Sony are fairly equal in quality. Sony is heavily invested in the digital camera world; they make their own sensors and they utilize Zeiss lenses on most of their point-and-shoots as well as on their digital SLRs.

Of course, you can't manage without carrying a tripod and a remote shutter release. Keep a tripod stashed in the trunk of your car. The remote release can be wireless or wired but it's a necessity for early morning and late evening shooting. This is prime time for the dramatic lighting that reveals coveted images. The tripod base needs to be sturdy, but don't invest in one you'd hate to lug up a hill. Very sturdy tripods are now made from carbon materials that are extremely light and strong. Tripod legs should be able to spread out so you can get the camera close to ground level. The tripod head is where convenience reigns. I find ball heads to be the quickest to adjust. Models with dual levels and a quick camera release are the most convenient.

Different cameras accept different media cards. Some cameras accept two different types of media cards. The most popular are SDHC cards (Secure Digital High Capacity) and CF cards (Compact Flash) . The cost for these cards decreases as bigger, faster versions are released. They come in different sizes and speeds. Some CF cards may say "Extreme III," which in some cases denotes a data transfer rate of 30 megabytes per second. Data on SDHC cards is protected even if the card is inserted into an incompatible device. SDHC-enabled products/card readers will work with any SD memory card.

The memory card is divided into memory units, and the host (camera) writes data onto areas where no data is already stored. As available memory becomes divided into smaller units through normal use, this can lead to fragmented storage, which can reduce write speeds or how quickly your camera accepts an image. Faster memory card speeds can help reduce data card fragmentation. Faster cards also allow you to shoot more quickly. When you take a picture, that data is downloaded into the camera's internal buffer. When that buffer becomes full, it then writes data to the card. If you are shooting many frames per second, the shutter may eventually stop firing as data transfer backs up. The faster the memory card, the faster the transfer of data from the camera. In addition, your images will upload more quickly to your computer with a faster card. Compact flash cards include error checking and correction. They are considered sturdier than other memory card formats. CFast is now the speed standard for CF cards.

Helpful as they are, memory cards can become corrupted when you turn off your camera or remove the card while performing a function on the camera. Corruption can happen over time, thanks to the constant deleting or simply to repeated usage. It's an excellent habit to reformat your cards occasionally to avoid this problem. You can do this in-camera or from your computer. And I've got to say it: be sure to save your images to your computer first. If your card does become corrupted and your hard-earned images appear lost to the ether, do not despair. There are myriad recovery software products that will resurrect your images in short order. I use PhotoRecovery and RescuePRO on my Mac. They work like a charm.

For this book I used a GPS/Geotagging device. There were occasions when the Geotagger battery died, so for those instances, I researched my GPS locations via Google Maps. Info is here for most images.

For shooting around my home landscape in the Carolina Lowcountry, I also recommend these essential bag contents: bug spray and a bottle of water. The best light often coincides with the onset of biting flies and mosquitoes. And when you're tromping around the subtropical countryside in search of the perfect shot, you'll certainly want to rehydrate.

Common Digital Camera Functions

Most amateur and professional cameras have a menu of camera functions that is accessed via a button on the camera and then viewed on the LCD screen. They are usually divided into camera, picture, set-up, and media card categories. Most of these you will never have the need to address. However, there are certain camera functions that are standard on even the most rudimentary point-and-shoot cameras.

Be sure to learn how to set your ISO. This will allow you to control image quality while shooting in various types of lighting situations. The lower the ISO, the better quality the im-

age, but you will need a bright light source in which to shoot. A higher ISO will let you shoot in that dark church but you will inevitably gain image noise (small black dots), and that becomes more evident as you enlarge the image.

Setting the resolution and file format at which you capture images is also paramount when you are concerned with image quality. Resolution refers to the number of pixels in an image; I'll address this in more detail later.

Learn how to tap the macro setting for close-ups of flowers, insects, etc. Be precise with your focus as you have very little margin for error shooting in the macro setting. You will do best to set the lens at its widest focal length and move the camera in and out to focus.

Know how to set the white balance of your camera. If you set it on Auto, you would fare well for most lighting situations. However, sometimes you will encounter inside (tungsten) light and daylight from a window. You can take an exposure reading of each light source to see which light is dominant and then set your camera for the proper color balance. This will prevent the people at the window from turning blue (if you're balanced for tungsten) or green, if you're shooting under fluorescent lights and balanced for daylight.

Digital Camera Care

Digital camera care starts with sensor cleaning. Your sensor's electromagnetic charge is, well, a magnet for any speck of dust that may pass its way. And while a speck of dust is pretty easily obliterated in a software-editing program, it's a lot easier to eradicate small blotches in a blue sky than to retouch a dark speck on someone's cheek. The healing brush in Lightroom or Photoshop works well here but it's always best if you just don't have any dust on the image. That begins with a clean sensor.

To see if your sensor is dust-free, attach a

lens that you know is free of dust. Open the lens to its widest f-stop and shoot a bright white background. Shooting the sky can work well here. Look at these high-resolution images on a computer and you will see any particles that may be on the sensor. In addition, there are many approaches and products for inspecting sensors. You can purchase a lighted, hand-held, or visor eyeglass magnifier. The visor magnifiers free up your hands to do some cleaning. However, they offer a very low level of magnification. The handheld magnifiers are more powerful, but sometimes you need a third hand or a clamp to hold the camera to clean it. With either type, just lock up the camera mirror and view the sensor through the vacant lens mount. That first peek will cost you at least 30 bucks for an Optivisor and up to $100 for a 7x Sensor Vu. These also come with a stand so you can look and clean simultaneously.

In reality you never actually clean the sensor itself, you clean a low pass filter mounted in front of the sensor. Some cameras can shake off the dust by vibrating thousands of times a second. That's the cheapest option but it's not the most effective approach. Others involve applying cleaning liquids with which you wipe away the dust, the swab and methanol method. However, this involves touching the sensor, which is always risky. In addition, methanol is highly flammable and is illegal on airplanes and in some countries.

An alternative is an electrostatic brush. Air passes through the brush and creates a charge on the bristles that attracts the dust. Be careful not to swipe any lubricants from adjoining hardware. Also, never touch the brush bristles or any cleaning utensil with your hand. Your skin contains oils that will adhere to the brush and transfer to your sensor. You can use a sticky adherent to pick dust off of the sensor, but only cleaning solutions will remove welded dust. In any event, never use compressed air to clean your sensor. It can spray moisture and chemical propellants that will damage the sensor. If the sensor is ruined, depending on the cost of your camera, you may as well buy a new camera. When it comes to dealing with such a fragile piece of equipment, choosing the right cleaning method is filled with compromise. Camera manufacturers will void your warranty if they see that you've dinged your sensor. In general, foot- or hand-powered blowers are your safest bet, although Photographic Solutions Inc. guarantees that you won't damage your camera if you use their Sensor Swabs and Eclipse.

The absolutely, unequivocally best site I've found for providing different cleaning techniques for digital camera sensors is, of course, www.cleaningdigitalcameras.com. These folks are camera repair people with a brick and mortar location and they want to help. They have tested most every cleaning concept and product and are the undisputed go-to guys for sensor-cleaning issues.

Hazards of the Southern climate

For photography fans, the Southeast conjures dreamy thoughts of strolling along a beach with camera in hand or a tripod set up by a marsh for taking an album's worth of beautiful images. It all sounds great until you start hearing a grinding sound when you change lenses or see dark spots on the interior of your lens. The grinding sound is surely caused by sand. The dark spots could be fungus growing inside the lens or simply a sprinkle of dust you collected. Shooting for extended periods in humid, hot, sunny, ocean and marsh locations puts your camera at risk to be damaged by salt, sand, heat, or direct sunlight. Here are a few quick tips to save the camera you love:

• Sand has an insidious nature and attacks your camera relentlessly. It's impossible to avoid its effects unless you keep your camera

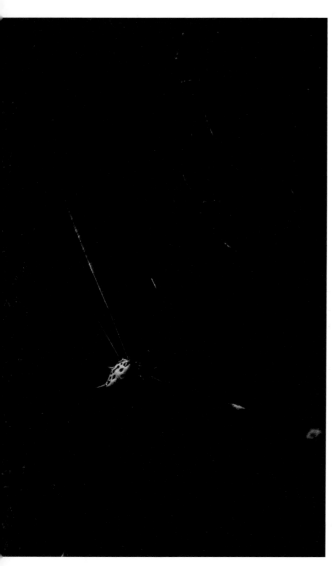

Spinybacked orbweaver, Lighthouse Overlook Trail. I should have used a ladder and a macro lens to get close but had to settle for my telephoto. GPS coordinates: 32°1'28" N, 80°53'4" W

in a protective housing, which is expensive, slow, and cumbersome to work with. Two Ziploc bags will do the trick in a pinch, or try the Waterproof Store (www.thewaterproof store.com) for a myriad of waterproofing and protective options. Your best defense against sand is to avoid changing lenses on the beach. Blow camera, lens, and camera bag thoroughly when you get inside and hope for the best.

• Salt is nefarious in that its corrosive effects are unseen until it's too late. Don't hang your camera around your neck after you've been in the ocean. Salt can transfer from your body, your clothes, or your hands and kick-start the corrosive process. Make sure every port on your camera is tightly sealed. Be sure to wipe down camera and lens with a slightly damp cloth to remove salt spray.

• Keep your camera lens away from direct sunlight. The jury is out on exactly how adverse the effects can be on your sensor, but avoidance is the safest practice. At the least, excessive heat can cause runny oils to contaminate your sensor or loosen the glues on some sensor packages. Camera sensors dump heat rapidly through radiation, and theories abound regarding sensor recrystallization, but it occurs only after prolonged exposure. Anyway, avoid carrying your camera on your tripod with the lens facing the sun.

• Water will kill anything electronic. Your camera and lens are no exceptions. If you happen to drop your camera into salt water, it's advisable to then immerse it into plain water to wash away the corrosive salt from inside it. It is then best to use a hair dryer on it at least until your heart palpitations ease. Place camera and lens in separate bags of rice to help draw out the moisture and get the camera to a professional repair shop. In some cases, the patient can be saved.

• Avoid keeping your camera in intense heat for too long a period. Excessive heat will melt your camera's lubricants, and you can do irreparable harm if you use the camera when it's too hot. Keep your camera bag under the seat of the air-conditioned car when traveling for long periods. For short hauls I leave the air conditioning off as my lens will fog when I go from an air-conditioned car to a humid exterior. The car's trunk beats the interior for camera storage during short hauls or when parked, but either option makes my palms sweat. You know that camera manual you always carry? It will tell you the maximum heat at which your camera can safely operate.

Composition and Exposure

There are certain rules of composition that can help make your photographs more interesting and more telling.

As you look at a square or rectangular "canvas," your eye moves from the bottom left of the frame to the top right, then to the top left and the bottom right. This all happens in a millisecond, but where you place the most important content effects the power of your image. Apply the rules of composition to elevate the expressiveness of your photographs.

The Rule of Thirds states that the human eye is drawn to an area that is about two thirds up the page. When shooting landscapes, depending on your area of emphasis, try to place your horizon line either at the bottom third or the top third of the frame. You will end up with either mostly sky or mostly ground in your image, as well as a photo with infinitely more interest than if you placed the horizon in the middle of the frame.

Whether it's a person, place, or thing, never put any area of interest in the exact middle of the frame. Photographs become static. It's like looking at someone with a line drawn down the middle of their face. You can't do it for more than a few seconds. You want to draw people into the image by placing areas of interest at the intersection of four lines that section the image into nine unequal parts. Each line is drawn so that the width of the resulting small part of the image relates to that of the big part exactly as the width of the whole image relates to the width of the big part. Did you make it through all that? (See diagram below.)

Leonardo da Vinci noticed that scenes with certain proportions are more pleasing to the human eye. Da Vinci called where the lines intersect the "golden points." Placing linear elements like fences, rivers, or roads on a diagonal within the frame gives the image a more active flow.

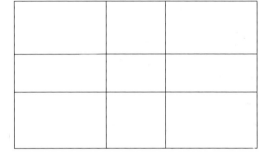

I had a photojournalism teacher who professed that most of your images should be visual verbs. Content and imagery should flow to create a story. Of course, you must use the rules to understand how best to break them. To paraphrase a photography master like Edward Weston, thinking too hard about rules of composition before taking a photograph is like considering the rules of gravity before taking a walk.

It's only natural for most folks to shoot on Program or Automatic modes, and it makes sense. Your exposures will be right on most of the time. You are free just to focus on your subject and not on the technical aspects of your

The two shots here of the couple are meant to demonstrate that there is usually more than one decent photo in a situation. Examine your compositions. I almost moved on before spotting the bird. GPS coordinates: 32°46'13" N, 79°51'43"

work. You can shoot in aperture preferred mode when you want to control depth of field. You can shoot in shutter preferred mode when you want to stop or blur the action.

There are, however, situations where it will behoove you to turn the exposure mode dial to manual. This is especially the case when shooting subjects that are backlit, exceptionally dark, or exceptionally bright. The light meter in your camera is calibrated to read a scene as being a neutral gray.

Discerning amateurs and many pros carry an 18 percent gray card from which to take a reflective meter reading. This exercise will give you the most accurate reading of the light hitting your subject. When your scene is on the bright side, your in-camera light meter will compensate and your exposure will tend to be dark. You need to overexpose a stop or so from your meter reading. The converse is true when your scene is on the dark side. Your images will be too light if you don't underexpose at least 1 f-stop.

Some cameras offer automatic exposure compensation that you can dial in or set via your camera's function menu. If there is a button on your camera with a plus or minus symbol, hold this down while turning the dial for an under- or overexposure value. Exposure usually changes in increments of $\frac{1}{3}$ of an f-stop, and this should be displayed on the LCD screen.

Automatic exposure compensation usually works best when using center-weighted or spot metering. Be careful here—it is unlikely that exposure value settings will be reset when the camera is turned off, but check your camera's manual.

The best solution for backlit subjects is to fill-flash your subject when possible. Try to keep the flash exposure about $\frac{1}{2}$ to 1 stop brighter than your ambient light reading. Your subject will pop out from the background.

Image Resolution and File Formats

Resolution is sometimes identified by the width and height of the image as well as the total number of pixels in it. The more megapixels on your camera sensor, the larger image you can make.

Determining the image size also determines how much the image can be manipulated. Many image file formats can be compressed to facilitate storage and file transfer. JPEG is called a *lossy* image compression medium because every time you compress the image, pixels are lost from the file. You can set most cameras to shoot with the JPEG compression algorithm.

Saving your image as a JPEG will reduce the file size and then you can decide how much you want to compress the image before saving it. When compressed at higher ratios, the block patterns in JPEGS are more evident and you can see a loss in image detail. This is especially true when you make prints larger than the file allows. The content of an image also determines how visible detail loss will be. An image with many similarly colored pixels can be compressed quite a bit without any noticeable loss of quality. A picture of a rainbow will pixelate much more quickly.

JPEGs are great when you want to reduce the image size and disk space required for storage while sacrificing only a small amount of image quality. The more you compress the same image however, the more the image quality suffers.

Formats such as BMP files do not compress the pixels in the image at all. TIFF files are larger than JPEG files and they preserve the integrity and quality of the image. TIFF files may be compressed or uncompressed. When compressed, the compression algorithm is lossless. The file gets smaller but it retains all the information.

Many people feel it is advantageous to capture the image as a RAW file. There are a few schools of thought regarding capturing images as JPEG files as opposed to RAW files. One incentive for shooting JPEG is that you can save more images to your memory card. Shooting JPEG is faster. Images are saved in the camera more quickly and they are quicker to work with on your PC. RAW files need to be converted to TIFF or JPEG before you can view or print them. You will need certain software that is capable of viewing RAW images, and there's always the danger that twenty years from now standards will have changed and your RAW images will no longer be readable on any PC or Mac. If you're confident that your images are well exposed and have the correct color balance, then you would do just as well to shoot JPEG.

If you feel that your shoot requires a bit of post-production image editing and you want to have the most flexibility when adjusting exposures, then I suggest shooting in the RAW format. You will inevitably convert your RAW files to 16-bit TIFF files, do all your processing, then convert to 8-bit files for printing. You lose nothing by shooting RAW except for a little time and the number of images you can fit on a memory card.

Photo Editing Software

Adobe Photoshop software for Mac or PC is the king of digital image editing software. It offers an abundant array of options for altering and correcting digital images in most any graphic format imaginable. The program is so deep, you could spend the remainder of your natural life exploring ways to perfect that underexposed shot of an alligator on the hunt.

At $699.00, Photoshop can melt your check card. Adobe Photoshop Elements offers a more cost-effective option for most image correction needs. At $99, it's a viable alternative to Photoshop.

The other arrow in your software quiver should be an image archiving and editing program like Adobe Lightroom or Apple's Aperture. They both offer great storage and tracking mechanisms. Both programs also offer image-editing capabilities that may be sufficient for many professional and most amateur shooters.

Lightroom is my preferred program for importing and organizing images, editing, and image manipulation. It allows me to rank, organize, and flag images and to create groups of images organized by these criteria.

There are two invaluable editing tools in Lightroom. First, the Exposure Brush allows you to paint an increase or decrease in exposure on any part of an image. If you don't like your initial attempt, just use the slider to correct your exposure. Flow, contrast, clarity, saturation, and brush size and density, are all editable. It's great for lightening a face or embellishing an entire scene.

You can edit RAW images in Lightroom and Aperture. All edits are nondestructive, and the original image remains intact.

Some of the top benefits of nondestructive images (NDI) include:

• Multiple photo manipulation: Digital cameras can produce large numbers of similar files in a way that scanning photos never could. Parametric image editing (PIE)—editing images by creating instructions or parameters for adjustment—makes it easy to apply settings from one photo to others very quickly.

• Unlimited undo: Since all image adjustments are saved simply as processing instructions, it's easy to change them and create a different interpretation of an image.

• Space savings: Since instructions are a lot smaller than pixels to store, the storage requirements are greatly reduced.

Lightroom and Aperture also accept plug-ins that access custom Photoshop filters. You can apply these editing effects in Lightroom without having to open the image in Photoshop. Plug-ins such as those from Imagenomic, Nik, and Extensis allow you to retouch skin tone, reduce image noise, sharpen images, and apply special effects. These procedures can be performed in Photoshop and custom plug-ins can be accessed from Photoshop as well. Plug-ins offer more options than comparable Photoshop filters and usually do a better job. Nik plug-ins allow you to alter a particular portion of an image. For instance, you can reduce digital noise in the sky, where it is more evident, while leaving adjacent areas untouched, thereby preserving sharpness.

Lightroom and Photoshop are comprehensive tools for organizing and manipulating your images. There are other choices but you can't go wrong with this duo.

Portable Flash

Most digital cameras come with some form of built-in flash. It always makes me laugh to see thousands of these going off in huge stadiums, the only effect being to blind the people directly in front of the cameras.

The light a flash emits must reflect off something to have an effect. Most in-camera flashes, even on high-end digital SLRs, don't do much good beyond 10 feet or so, but no software tool will fill in your dark subject without adding unacceptable image problems.

If you want to fill in the shadows in a shadowy Savannah alley or on the face of a backlit basket weaver, you've got to use a more powerful form of auxiliary light. You are more easily identified as a "real" photographer when using a powerful flash. It's hard to be stealthy while emitting blasts of light, but you get the shot and get it right, in-camera.

Most portable flashes can be set to fire while the camera is on Manual mode, or you can set it to fire on Automatic and Automatic TTL for optimum fill-in flash. I recommend trying the latter while using your camera's Program setting. This takes the guesswork out of flash exposures and allows you to just shoot. Exposures will be right on for most situations. Set an ISO of 400 or 800 and you should do well. At night, use a tripod.

It's advisable to spend some time with your flash manual. Afterward, you will probably be good to go and can blast away. That's part of the beauty of digital—you can experiment till your battery drains and it costs you nothing.

I do recommend using a flash brand similar to your camera brand. It's not a hard-and-fast rule, but manufacturers include so many pro-

I would often see this woman on Front Beach, Isle of Palms, walking her dogs and carrying a chair that she would plop into every 100 yards or so. When lighting portraits, try to keep the background lighter on the shadow side and darker on the lit side to enhance contrast. GPS coordinates: 32°47'1" N, 79°47'31" W

prietary functions (not to mention cables) that your photographic life will be immeasurably easier if you use complementary equipment brands. You may like the features on that Canon flash but I guarantee it's not a good fit for your Nikon DSLR. The hot shoe hardware must correspond to the camera electronics to work on anything other than a manual setting.

With the advent of more sophisticated sensor production many pros are forgoing the use of flash altogether. The "noise" produced on an image is usually intensified when a photo is shot at a high ISO in a dark setting. It has a lot to do with the hot pixel charge exceeding the linear charge capacity of the sensor, but that is beyond the scope of this book.

Suffice it to say that advances in digital camera sensor production have made improvements that transcend camera noise issues. High-end DSLRs from Canon and Nikon are now capable of shooting at ISOs of 1600 and 3200 without objectionable noise issues.

Software filters like Imagenomic's Noiseware and Photoshop's Image Layering tone down objectionable digital noise. Combine three or more images of the same scene for optimum results. When layering images, use the Median setting if the camera was handheld and the Mean setting if you used a tripod.

GPS and Map Location Display

Geotagging is the process of adding geographical identification (metadata) to various media, such as photographs. These data typically include date, time, shutter speed, aperture, and other image-related data. There is also space for GPS data, which consists of latitude and longitude coordinates (and may also include altitude, bearing, distance, accuracy data, and place names). When you take a photo with a GPS-capable camera, this information is automatically added to the photograph in the form of an EXIF File.

I have a geotagging device from Easytag Technologies (www.e-geotag.com) that's made for my Nikon and attaches to a proprietary GPS port on the side of my D90. The Easytag has a built-in battery that lasts ten hours and then taps your camera battery if it runs low (though mine has died occasionally). It is charged via any powered USB port. The Easytag attaches to a camera's hot shoe and allows the camera's built-in flash to operate normally. It takes less than a minute to set it up. Once it locks onto a GPS satellite, you're golden (until you head indoors or turn the unit off). If you move inside and leave the unit on, it will memorize the last location fix and send this location to the camera until GPS signals are again received from the satellite.

The Easytag accepts a 2-gigabyte mini SD card to store thousands of waypoints or trail locations. These locations can be uploaded to Google Earth or Google Maps and added to web sites such as Flickr, panoramio, Picasa, and Locr. You will be able to see the path you traveled, the location where each photo was taken, and a small rendition of the photo. Plugins for Lightroom and Aperture allow you to upload photos directly to sharing websites, although Easytag comes with free uploading software. The Easytag will also work with point-and-shoot cameras and JPEG, TIFF, and RAW formats are supported.

There are web sites and attending software like EveryTrail (www.everytrail.com) which also work with camera phones (and standalone GPS units). With the EveryTrail Pro app you can search for nearby trips, follow a trip on your phone, and download EveryTrail mobile travel guides for your next adventure. It's an ideal technology for walking tours, biking, running, hiking, sailing, driving, and much more.

You can even see your route mapped out while your trip is in progress.

EveryTrail is also available for iPhone, BlackBerry, Android, and Windows Mobile uses. Just install their free custom application and activate your phone's GPS capabilities to track your trip route. Take pictures with your phone's camera and they'll automatically be plotted on your map. Camera phones are the wave of the future. They are catching up to point-and-shoot camera quality.

Camera Phones

I'm touching on the subject of the camera phone because many times it's the only camera you will have available. Great strides have been made in the quality of camera phones. The latest devices offer 12-megapixel sensors, and many models offer zoom lenses and a flash.

Everyone seems to be hung up on their camera's megapixel count. Apparently, you can't be too rich, too thin, or have too many megapixels. Yet packing so many megapixels on the small sensor of a camera phone or a small point-and-shoot device can be a decided detriment. In August 2010, Canon released a 120-megapixel sensor. However, jamming more pixels into a sensor is not necessarily going to provide higher-quality photographs. In fact, packing more light-sensitive pixels into a tiny sensor can result in greater noise in the photos, especially when images are shot at low light levels. Noise-reduction features can be found in many software programs, and noise-reduction plug-ins for Adobe Photoshop offer the best results. Remember, always reduce noise first and then sharpen your image.

Faster CPUs, advanced image-processing algorithms, and features such as image stabilization, high ISO settings, geotagging, and instant upload to the Web have made some camera phones downright superior to many point-and-shoot cameras. The 8-megapixel Samsung Memoir T929 actually looks like a camera and has grips placed where it's best to hold the phone while taking pictures. An included widget allows you to upload photographs to sharing services like Photobucket and Flickr with a single click—you don't even need to launch an application. The phone supports geotagging to archive and display all your photos and provide the exact map location where they were shot from. The camera captures images at resolutions up to 3,264 x 2,448 pixels and stores them on a MicroSD card. The image quality is excellent. You can zoom in up to 8X. In addition, there are 12 preset modes and it will cobble together a series of photos to produce a panoramic shot.

A few things to consider when using a camera phone: The shutter lag can be reminiscent of point-and-shoots from a few years ago. Sometimes the picture is gone by the time the shutter—and your patience—snap. Be mindful of camera shake too; longer shutter speeds require steadier hands. A little practice goes a long way here.

All the images in the montage on page 12 were made as part of a personal project to shoot in the same location at the same time of day for two months. I was trying to force myself to look at familiar objects in a new way and to try and come away with fresh images at each visit. Alfred Steiglitz attempted the same exercise in a controlled environment with a simple teacup. He lit and composed this mundane item in as many ways he could devise as an exercise in seeing. It was in many ways a metaphor for his life and career.

The camera phone is a great safety valve. Get a good one and play. It's not the equipment, it's your eye that's critical.

I. Summerville

www.summerville.sc.us

Cool breezes, majestic pine trees, and welcome respite from subtropical South Carolina summers—that's the combination that sent Charlestonians of old packing to the healing climes of Summerville.

These days, if you head west, up I-26, about 20 miles from Charleston, toward Columbia, SC, you will approach the exit (199A) for Summerville, SC.

The town's center has the charm of a Norman Rockwell painting. Live oaks dripping with Spanish moss line streets with cottages and country stores; nineteenth-century gabled homes and sweeping verandas conjure up images of families sipping iced tea under rattan fans.

A spring to fall farmers' market accentuates the relaxed pace of this peaceful burg. Catch it while you can, as the area is growing and expanding quickly.

In Summerville, the influx of newcomers has spawned an entrepreneurial spirit that produces new businesses in well-designed pedestrian malls and piazzas. Art galleries, antiques shops, an eclectic selection of restaurants, cafés, artisan shops, designer clothing stores, and myriad services create the delicate dance of small-town life. Summerville is a great point

Azalea Park has gone through many incarnations since its inception 68 years ago. It was started by a group of women called the Civic League, a precursor to the Garden Club of Summerville. The park is at the corner of West 5th South Street. **Follow the Leader** *is a set of bronze sculptures by W. Sandy Proctor.* GPS coordinates: 33°0'55" N, 80°10'50" W

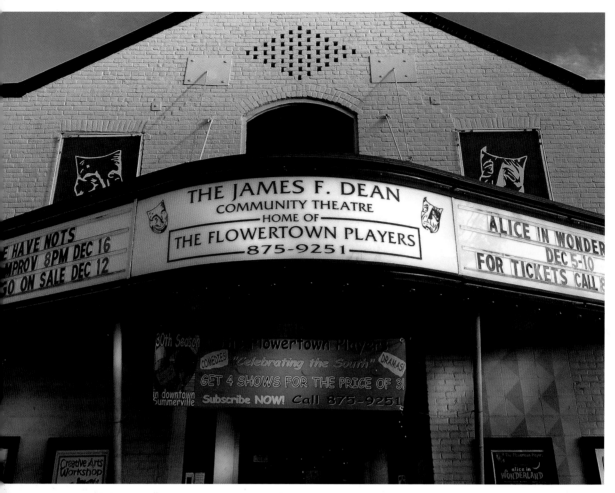

James F. Dean Community Theater, originally the Theatre on the Square in downtown Summerville, was built in 1935 and operated as a movie house until the early 1960s. The theater is listed on the National Register of Historic Places. GPS coordinates: 33°1'8" N, 80°10'33" W

of departure for sojourns south to Charleston and beyond.

Where: Located 20 miles west of Charleston, SC. Take Exit 199A off of I-26.

Noted for: Summerville is noted for its relatively cooler climate, classic "Southern" neighborhoods and architecture, and Guerin's Pharmacy, the oldest continuing business in South Carolina. If you're in town at the beginning of April, be sure to catch the Flowertown

Festival. The main attraction is more than 200 jury-selected artisans from throughout the country who pitch their tents in Azalea Park and on Main Street.

What to Watch for: Main Street is bisected by a well-landscaped town square called Hutchinson Square; it hosts a variety of exhibits throughout the year that champion various holiday seasons. The Christmas display is particularly dazzling.

Right: Cypress Gardens is located 20 minutes west of Summerville, in Moncks Corner. There's an aviary, a butterfly garden, and the Swamparium at Cypress Gardens, but the real fun is taking a ride in a flat-bottom swamp boat through a black-water bald cypress swamp. The guides love to tell you about the scene from the movie The Patriot *that was shot in the swamp.* GPS coordinates: 33°3'11" N, 79°56'44"

Below: Guerin's Pharmacy, a treasured time cap-sule, is located on the west side of Main Street and is the oldest continuing business in Summerville as well as the oldest pharmacy in South Carolina. GPS coordinates: 33°1'9" N, 80°10'34" W

Saints Cyril & Methodius Orthodox Church (122 South Main St.) is a parish of the Russian Orthodox Church Abroad. The site was the original location of the Salisbury Theater, a blacks-only movie theater that operated in the 1940s and '50s. Streaks of light stream through a row of skylights. GPS coordinates: 33°1'11" N, 80°10'33" W

Above: Interesting architectural details abound on Summerville streets.

Right top: Architectural details on Tupper Lane, just out of town, headed south on Main Street.

Right bottom: Earthquake bolts are the outer washers and nuts of strengthening rods inserted through older buildings to help keep them erect. GPS coordinates: 33°1'10" N, 80°10'34" W

The marsh is a popular fishing and crabbing destination. This view from the Pitt Street Bridge includes a marina and the Ben Sawyer Bridge in the distant background. GPS coordinates: 32°46'16" N, 79°51'44"

II. Mount Pleasant

www.townofmountpleasant.com

Sewee Indians were the first known residents of Mount Pleasant. The Sewee population was about 800 in the year 1600, and they met their first white man when the ship *Carolina* arrived with English settlers in 1670.

The name "Mount Pleasant" comes from the plantation once owned by Jacob Motte. When James Hibben bought the Mount Pleasant property from Jacob Motte in 1803, he moved into Motte's home at 111 Hibben Street. The Hibben House is the oldest home in the City of Mount Pleasant.

By 1885, Mount Pleasant was known as a retreat and resort for the pleasure and health of the populace of Charleston. Today it is a vibrant suburb that was recently named one of the 10 fastest-growing communities in the country.

Where: From Summerville, take Highway 26 East to Highway 526 East. Merge right when you see the sign for Exit 29, Georgetown. You will land smack in the middle of Mount Pleasant. Turn right onto Highway 17 to get to the Ravenel Bridge or turn left to head to the Isle of Palms Connector. From downtown Charleston take the Ravenel Bridge or a $6 water taxi from the Charleston Maritime Center to Mount Pleasant.

Noted for: At the base of the Ravenel Bridge lies Patriots Point, the maritime and naval museum that is home to the aircraft carrier USS *Yorktown*. The *Yorktown* is a museum ship with a rich history; it's the largest tourist attraction in the state.

Boone Hall Plantation is an interesting albeit pricey place to visit. However, Boone Hall

In 1975, the USS Yorktown *(CV-10) was towed to Patriots Point to become the main attraction of the new Patriots Point Naval and Maritime Museum. Get to Patriots Point in the morning, when the front of the ship is lit by the rising sun. Bring a flash for interior shots as available lighting is sparse and dominated by single light bulbs. GPS coordinates: 32°47'25" N, 79°54'20" W*

does have a classic avenue of oaks and historically important slave cabins on site.

What to Watch for: Mount Pleasant offers an array of festivals and events that cater to families and new friends. The January Lowcountry Oyster Festival, the seasonal farmers' market on Coleman Boulevard, autumn's Taste of Charleston food festival, and the spring Blessing of the Fleet events all afford ample opportunities to snag great pictures. The Blessing of the Fleet honors the area's diminishing shrimping industry in the third week of April. It's held at the Mount Pleasant Waterfront Park and attracts more than 10,000 attendees each year.

Prior to the Revolutionary War, a plank bridge set on barrels was constructed to span Cove Inlet and connect Mount Pleasant with Sullivan's Island. Today, this truncated version of the Pitt Street Bridge is a great spot for 4th of July fireworks photos as you get unrestricted views of the Intracoastal Waterway, Sullivan's Island, the Charleston peninsula skyline, Charleston Harbor, Isle of Palms, James Island, Folly Beach, and all their fireworks displays.

Don't miss the small details that might make a great photo. GPS coordinates: 32°49'29" N, 79°48'47" W

Above: Egrets and ibis gather in the early morning light off the Isle of Palms Connector. The connector joins US-17 in Mount Pleasant with SC-703 on the Isle of Palms. Pull over anywhere on the connector to photograph the incredible array of birds as well as the occasional human presence. GPS coordinates: 32°23'16" N, 80°34'33" W

Left: This nest is occupied by osprey or owls every spring. It's on the 3-mile-long Isle of Palms Connector (Highway 517) and rests on a telephone pole just before you reach the marsh. You can also visit the Avian Conservation Center/The Center for Birds of Prey (www.thecenterforbirdsofprey .org), at 4872 Sewee Rd., Awendaw, SC 29429 to learn more. Demonstrations offer the chance to photograph falcons, turkey vultures, owls, bald eagles, and other raptors. GPS coordinates: 32°48'58" N, 79°48'33" W

Palmetto Islands County Park is a 943-acre park abutting a huge marshland on one side and residential areas on the other. The park's truly subtropical setting attracts every form of wildlife that can access this pat of butter in a plate of grits. There's a 50-foot observation tower that overlooks a great expanse of marshland. Unless you're creating a purely artistic piece or are blessed with a beautiful sunset, find a focal point in your photos to generate interest in landscapes with a huge expanse of ground and horizon. GPS coordinates: 32°51'44" N, 79°49'37" W

Hibben House is the oldest residence in Mount Pleasant. It is now a private home, so if you decide to take a photo, you must take it from the street. GPS coordinates: 32°47'16" N, 79°52'49" W

You will run into Shem Creek if you take the Mount Pleasant/Sullivan's Island exit on the Ravenel Bridge. Vickery's Shem Creek restaurant has a small bar where they'll put a refreshing drink in one of your hands while you use the cable release in the other. The bar area offers stellar views of the marsh, docked shrimp boats, kayakers, and the thoroughfare filled with boats heading in and out of Charleston harbor. A phantasmagoric scene of dolphins, pelicans, egrets, boaters, jet skiers, board paddlers, and creekside diners make this my hands-down favorite place to be in Mount Pleasant. GPS coordinates: 32.°47'31" N, 79°52'57" W

III. Isle of Palms

www.iop.net

The Isle of Palms was originally called Hunting Island, and it is known to have been around for at least 25,000 years.

Now a location for beachgoers and second-home owners, IOP, as it is called, was reportedly the repository of buried pirate treasure (though no doubloon has yet been found), and was rumored to be the resting place of gangster Francis "Duke" Connelly's ill-gotten gains.

The Isle of Palms is one of the thirty-five South Carolina barrier islands (the state is second only to Florida in the number of islands), which absorb the brunt of tidal surges from storms. But IOP was outmatched in 1989 when the eye of Hurricane Hugo passed directly overhead.

The Isle of Palms has recovered quite nicely from those days. The Clean Beaches Coalition, which certifies beaches as clean and environmentally sound, recognizes Isle of Palms as a Blue Wave Beach.

A three-block commercial area runs along the island's Front Beach, bookended by a

The pier at Isle of Palms is the focal point of Front Beach and a good spot to shoot around for portraits. (Play it safe with portraits. If you think you might publish or sell a portrait or a shot with people in it—any shot where someone's face is clear and he or she could be identified—you must have a signed release form from your subject. Free model release forms can be found online.) Mornings and late evenings are a good time to shoot the fishermen, pelicans, cormorants, osprey, and the surfers who ply the surrounding waters. The sun rises on the northern side of the pier but I like shooting on the backlit, shadowy side. GPS coordinates: 32°47'7" N, 79°47'16" W

Sunrise, Isle of Palms, Front Beach; GPS coordinates: 32°47'6" N, 79°47'13" W

county park on one end and residential neighborhoods on the other. Isle of Palms Marina, located on the east side of the Intracoastal Waterway, is a jumping-off point for Dewees and Capers islands. Dewees is an environmentally sustainable development. Capers is an unspoiled spit of land visited often by local boaters.

On the southern end of the island, be sure to visit the upstairs bar at the Boathouse Restaurant. This aerie offers amazing views of the ocean, Breach Inlet, and the Intracoastal. You'll see dolphins, sea birds, and gorgeous sunsets.

Where: The Isle of Palms can be reached from US 17 East, by turning right onto Highway 517 or the Isle of Palms Connector. Isle of Palms is a straight shot, 3.5 miles across a beautiful salt marsh that will constantly tempt you to pull over to shoot a flock of storks or an osprey on one of its trips to fish in the ocean.

Noted for: The area is known for the Isle of Palms County Park, located near Front Beach. Just go straight as you come off of the Connector. Pier access is limited to guests of the condo development there, but you'll find interesting shots around its base.

Isle of Palms is also known as the embarkation point for the CSS *H. L. Hunley,* the first submarine (Confederate) ever to sink an enemy ship. Lost at sea for 130 years with all its crew members, the sub was raised from the sea floor in 2000. Visitors are welcome at the recovery lab in North Charleston; regrettably, no photography is permitted during the tour.

What to Watch for: The Island Turtle Team (www.ccgnet.com/turtleteam) is a group of volunteers that tracks and monitors endangered loggerhead sea turtle nests during their May to October nesting season. There are similar groups all along the Southeast coast, where an estimated 14,000 female sea turtles nest each year.

Turtle hatchlings are disoriented by artificial light, which can lead them away from the ocean to what appears to be a full moon. That's why the beloved Ravenel Bridge and local beach houses go dark on summer evenings.

When photographing nesting mothers or hatchlings at night, you are really swimming upstream photographically. Don't use a white light flash. Don't let your work affect the turtles at all. Infrared is inconvenient and impractical for shooting night shots of moving hatchlings but it is certainly the environmentally correct way to go.

Your best solution here may entail purchasing a new camera. You can find an infrared digital camera with an infrared flash that is undetectable. These are mostly used for shooting photos of game animals at night, but they are a good solution to the turtle conundrum.

The sea turtle/infrared camera scenario is a great example of why photographers may want to learn more than what the Automatic dial on their cameras can provide. The photographic process is almost always a give and take between your camera and equipment, what is offered by your environment, and what you are trying to achieve in the photo. Learn what your camera can do and think about what outcome you are trying to achieve. Unless you're in a controlled lighting situation you will never have power over your environment, so think about f-stops and shutter speed and how they can help you produce the photographic image you desire.

Early morning, Isle of Palms pier; GPS coordinates: 32°47'4" N, 79°47'18" W

One of many designer mailboxes on the island; GPS coordinates: 32°46'2" N, 79°49'23" W

IV. Sullivan's Island

www.sullivansisland-sc.com

The second group of settlers to land in Charleston included an Irishman named Florence O'Sullivan, from whom Sullivan's Island took its name.

Sullivan's Island's position at the entrance to Charleston Harbor anointed it as Charleston's first naval line of defense. Colonel William Moultrie placed thirty-one guns at Fort Moultrie during the Revolutionary War, and the practice of placing big guns on Sullivan's Island continued during WWII. Fort Moultrie developed a large gunnery range that extended from Station 28½ down to Breach Inlet. During World War II, these guns were meant to protect troops as they shipped out overseas.

Sullivan's Island never developed any long-standing commercial industries; its main attractions were and are its beaches and its breezes. Vacation home rentals and boarding houses are its "cottage" industry.

Be sure to visit Station 28 and the gun placement pictured on page 49. The cement outcrop has been buried by sand and silt carried down from the mountains. The sand dumps into the harbor and is blocked by man-made jetties at Folly Beach, which ricochet it back to Sullivan's Island. The result: Sullivan's

Beachfront house supports hold a well-traveled float. GPS coordinates: 32°46'6" N, 79°49'1" W

Island has actually grown through accretion in recent years, while many barrier islands suffer from erosion. The gun placement will eventually become buried, so get there soon to take a look and a photo.

Where: From southern Mount Pleasant and Coleman Boulevard, head over the Intracoastal Waterway on the Ben Sawyer Bridge and alight onto the three-block-long town of Sullivan's Island. From north of Mount Pleasant, head over the Isle of Palms Connector and make your first right turn. Head straight on Palm Boulevard, and when you cross the Breach Inlet Bridge, you've landed on Sullivan's Island.

Noted for: Sullivan's Island is noted for its vast, beautiful expanse of beach, which runs the entire length of the island. The beach has excellent wind resistance—it even withstood Hurricane Hugo's category 4 winds. The island has the only lighthouse with both an elevator and siding, and on a clear night it can be seen from as far as 27 miles at sea. Unfortunately, only its base is open to the public.

Fort Moultrie on Sullivan's is a unit of Fort Sumter National Monument. The fort has played a part in Southern naval defense for over 170 years. The fort was constructed mostly of palmetto trees, and the soft nature of the wood prevented injury from splinters when

Bunker and gun placements, Fort Moultrie, Sullivan's Island; GPS coordinates: 32°45'35" N, 79°51'32" W

Sullivans Island Lighthouse; GPS coordinates: 32°45'24" N, 79°50'35" W

the fort was bombarded. Edgar Allan Poe was stationed at Fort Moultrie and wrote "The Gold Bug" there.

What to Watch for: There are a number of beautiful churches on Sullivan's Island. Stella Maris on Middle Street is worth a look. You can follow the church bells right to its front door.

Sullivan's Island's downtown area starts at Station 22 and is about three blocks long. Grab a bite at Poe's or High Thyme. In addition, there's a park at the end of town where you can go to gather yourself after a morning's shoot.

Tide pools form at high tide near Station 22. GPS
coordinates: 32°45'39" N, 79°50'7" W

Beachfront World War II gun placement near Station 28. You can still see the gears on which the gun was moved. GPS coordinates: 32°46'4" N, 79°49'3" W

This hammock sits on a point overlooking the ocean. When an image has a lot of sky, be sure to increase your exposure from your meter reading, otherwise the meter will overcorrect and you'll have an under-exposed image. GPS coordinates: 32°46'10" N, 79°48'55" W

Above: Paddleboarder at Station 28½, Sullivan's Island; GPS coordinates: 32°45'58" N, 79°49'12" W

Right: This sign is just over the Breach Inlet Bridge that separates Isle of Palms from Sullivan's Island. Swimming the Breach Inlet waterway is potentially lethal, but it's a great place to photograph dolphins that are headed to the marsh inlets to feed. GPS coordinates: 32°46'31" N, 79°48'49" W

Balcony detail; GPS coordinates: 32°46'25" N, 79°55'38" W

V. Charleston

www.cityofcharleston.org

We could devote an entire book to the Charleston peninsula, or to its gardens, its historic homes, or even to its firsts. Charleston is rich in stories. For instance, Charleston registered the first Reform Jewish congregation and the oldest synagogue in the United States. The Dock Street Theater was the first building in the United States constructed to be used exclusively as a theater. In addition, Charleston boasts:

- The first public museum in the United States
- The oldest municipal Chamber of Commerce still in operation
- The first independent government in the colonies
- The first golf club
- The first cotton mill
- The first building to be used solely as a college library
- The first state to fire a shot in the Civil War
- The first submarine to sink an enemy ship in battle
- The first state to secede from the Union

Charleston also holds some notable repeat honors. *Condé Nast Traveler* magazine has named Charleston America's Friendliest City for many years. It also named Charleston Americas Best City to Visit for the third successive year in 2010, second only to perennial winner San Francisco.

This city is rich in photography subjects. You won't run into the big-city obstacles that prevent you from placing a tripod on the steps of City Hall or lying on the sidewalk to get an ant's-eye view of St. Michael's Church steeple. Charleston's polite denizens will likely form a protective ring around you, shield the sun from your lens, and ask you how they can help.

Charleston is a walking city. With a comfortable pair of shoes you can canvas the peninsula over the course of a couple of days. Visually, the most interesting area is "South of Broad." The historic, residential neighborhoods to the south of Broad Street occupy the southern third of the peninsula. They contain cobblestone, gas-lit streets, tiny byways and alleys, and a collection of historic, antebellum architecture that will have you burning through 16-gig media cards in no time.

Meander down to the southern tip of the peninsula to White Point Gardens, named for the swell of white oyster shells that originally made up the earth here. A small park with live oaks, Civil War cannons, statues, and a gazebo flank the High Battery, a promenade with a panoramic view of the Charleston harbor and Fort Sumter. Listen closely and you'll swear you hear the gallows creaking under the weight of pirates and other villains.

It's fun to photograph the replica cannon and the welded mound of cannon balls. The nearby mansions offer good architectural details, and the Nathaniel Russell House (circa 1809) is usually open for a visit. Head up East Bay Street to visit mansions built by cotton and indigo merchants. Of special merit: The Edmond-Alston House and the Palmer House, also known as the Pink Palace.

Charleston is a wonderful "studio" for all photographers. The light is gorgeous—we credit that to the city's position on the water, its shady blocks, and the play of color in the

Window detail on Meeting Street. The dappled effects of sun shining through live oaks is like having a cookaloris with you throughout the day. A cookaloris is a solid sheet of any material in which you cut a random pattern to shine a light through to break up backgrounds. GPS coordinates: 32°46'20" N, 79°55'49" W

city's built environment. Catch quintessential images of the Holy City in its park squares, fountains, wrought iron gates, houses of worship, historic homes, and flowering gardens.

Where: From Sullivan's Island, head to Station 22½, where you will find Ben Sawyer Boulevard and the newly renovated Ben Sawyer Bridge. The small swing-span bridge overlooks the intracoastal waterway; travel over it and in 20 seconds you'll be in the lovely burgh of Mount Pleasant.

Directly on the Mount Pleasant side is Gold Bug Island, a 200-yard dollop of sand where Edgar Allen Poe set much of his short story "The Gold Bug." There's a spot here that hosts local events, and it is also a good site to stop and shoot marsh life (if the front gate is open).

Depart Gold Bug Island, continue on to Coleman Boulevard, and head across the Ravenel Bridge to Charleston. You can walk the bridge on its pedestrian lane to grab shots of the historic harbor.

Across the bridge, take the first exit to East Bay for the quickest entrée to downtown. This street winds down the side of the peninsula, providing easy access to the city market, picturesque East Bay, South of Broad, and White Point Gardens.

Noted for: Charleston is known as the Holy City, due to the seemingly uncountable number of churches that populate the tri-county area. Charleston was also one of the few cities in the original 13 colonies that practiced religious tolerance.

The city is also known for the Charleston Single House, a residential design that is one room wide and two stories high, with two piazzas that offer cross-ventilating relief from the hot, humid climate. The narrow end of these houses faces the street and the two porches located on the long side are perfect for lounging by the garden.

Local custom has it that an open porch door indicates the occupants are accepting callers. And while locals remain very gracious—in spite of often finding tourists crawling (literally) all over their homes and gardens—the open-door policy is largely a thing of the past.

What to Watch for: If you visit at the end of May, you will encounter Charleston's busiest period. Credit largely goes to the Spoleto Festival USA (www.spoletousa.org/home), a 14-day performing arts extravaganza that takes over the city. It's a great time to visit. Photography is permitted for some venues but not others. A letter to the Spoleto offices may grant permission to shoot rehearsals.

You may want to coordinate your visit to Charleston with the Cooper River 10K Bridge Run (www.bridgerun.com/index.php). Inaugurated in 1978, the race winds from Mount Pleasant to downtown Charleston on the first Saturday in April.

Eclipsing the Bridge Run and Spoleto for the busiest seasonal event is the Southeast Wildlife Exposition (www.sewe.com). With more than 40,000 visitors, 500 artists and exhibitors, and the worlds' most renowned experts on wildlife, conservation, and environmental issues, it has become the largest event of its kind in the nation. You can photograph alongside some of the nation's best ornithologists, shoot a birds-of-prey demonstration, and capture fly-fishing, cast net, and retriever demonstrations over the course of the three-day event.

You will often find children selling handmade sweetgrass flowers throughout the downtown area. Sweetgrass basketweavers are notoriously camera shy. They don't like to have their pictures taken, so please ask first. If you are wise enough to purchase one of their baskets, they may let you snap a frame. Sweetgrass baskets are watertight when made well. **GPS coordinates: 32°46'14" N, 79°55'42" W**

Top left: Feel free to cool off in the circular, multi-jet fountain downtown at Waterfront Park. The Park has won awards from the American Society of Landscape Architects and the National Trust for Historic Preservation. There's a long pier that stretches into the Cooper River. You have great views of the Yorktown *aircraft carrier and the Ravenel Bridge. To the right, about halfway down the park's half-mile length, is the Pineapple Fountain (and a second chance to take a dip). The pineapple is a symbol of hospitality, and bathers are welcome here.* GPS coordinates: 32°46'44" N, 79°55'31" W

Left, bottom: Cookaloris effect on a Dash Trolley; GPS coordinates: 32°47'17" N, 79°56'15" W

Above: Wrought iron terrace, 8 Meeting Street, Charleston; GPS coordinates: 32°46'15" N, 79°55'48" W

Left: Revolutionary war hero Major General William Moultrie stands guard in White Point Gardens, the Battery. You need a powerful flash unit to fill in on a black statue. I had to open up and overexpose the sky a bit to get any detail on the statue. GPS coordinates: 32°46'10" N, 79°55'43" W

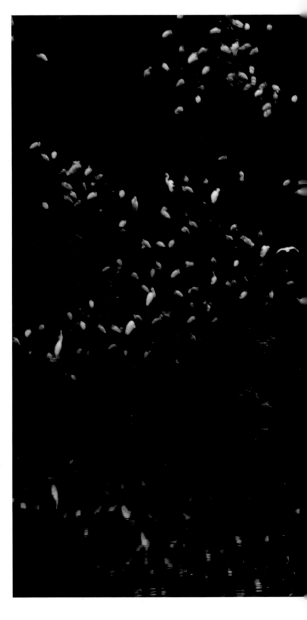

This classic Charleston scene is played out on the corner of East Battery and South Battery. The building appears to be leaning toward the background. This is called keystoning and can be fixed within software. Be careful when doing so: If your camera angle is very low or very high, your mind expects to see this convergence. If you correct the building lines so they are parallel to the edge of your print, the top of the building may appear wider. It diverges from our usual experience so be judicial in all your corrections. GPS coordinates: 32°46'12" N, 79°55'42" W

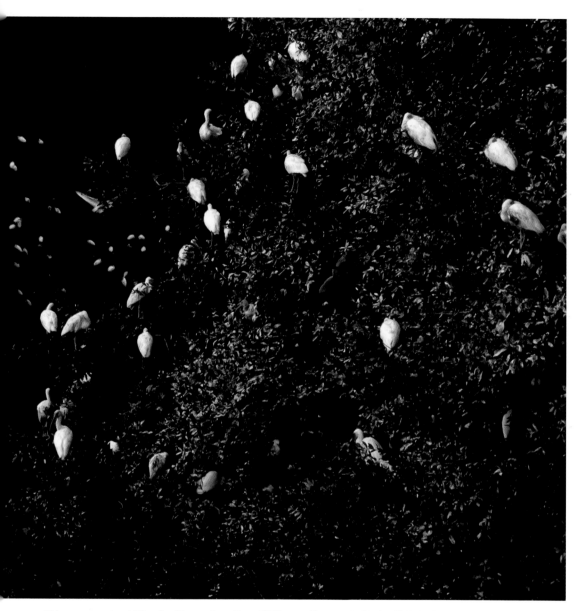

Ibis congregate at Charles Towne Landing; GPS coordinates: 32°48'24" N, 79°59'25" W

Right top: Private garden, Meeting Street; GPS coordinates: 32°46'14" N, 79°55'49" W

Right bottom: Muscadine grapes at the Charleston Farmers Market, one of the best in the country. You might also take a 20-minute ride to the Irvin House Vineyards on Wadmalaw Island. It's the only winery in Charleston, and they grow the grapes, harvest them, make the wine, and bottle it all on-site. GPS coordinates: 32°47'12" N, 79°56'12" W

Below: Doorbell of the Calhoun Mansion on Meeting Street. The 24,000-square-foot structure is the largest family residence in Charleston. GPS coordinates: 32°46'17" N, 79°55'49" W

St. Mathews Lutheran Church towers over midday sun worshippers in Marion Square. (I did not do any lens correction here.) GPS coordinates: 32°47'11" N, 79°56'5" W

Pier, Folly Beach; GPS coordinates: 32°39'17" N, 79°56'25" W

VI. Folly Beach

www.follybeachsouthcarolina.org
www.cityoffollybeach.com

There are quite a few theories as to how Folly Beach, previously Folly Island, got its name. Perhaps it was named for bodies that washed ashore from the Coast of Folly shipwreck. Once named Coffin Island, Folly used to serve as quarantine for sick passengers trying to enter the port of Charleston.

Today, it's one of the Lowcountry's most bohemian locales, proudly proclaiming itself the Edge of America. The surfer mentality that oozes through the little town doesn't hint at Folly's serious beginnings.

In the 1860s, cadets from the Citadel fired the first shots of the Civil War from nearby Morris Island, a state preserve with a lighthouse listed on the National Register of Historic Places. Three months later, the more famous shots were fired on Fort Sumter from James Island's Fort Johnson.

By the early 1930s, just nine families lived on the island year-round. In 1934, George Gershwin stayed at 708 West Arctic and wrote *Porgy and Bess*.

Where: A barrier island, Folly Beach is located 20 minutes from downtown Charleston, just between the Folly River and the Atlantic Ocean. From the Charleston peninsula head over to Lockwood Drive and take the James Island Connector to the end. Make a left onto Folly Road and head straight until you see the hotel on the beach. You've arrived at the edge of America.

Noted for: Folly Beach is noted for its surf scene and bohemian lifestyle, however, the allure of beachfront property has attracted a

Morris Island Lightouse with Folly Beach in the background; GPS coordinates: 32°39'17" N, 79°56'25" W

moneyed crowd who currently share space with the surfers and their young tribe. Visit www.follysurfcam.com to check out the surf conditions.

Folly Beach is the site of many loggerhead sea turtle nests. Every summer, female loggerhead turtles return to the same beaches where they were born to dig a nest and lay their eggs.

The Folly Beach Turtle Watch Program counts nests and monitors the seasonal activity.

What to Watch for: In the winter the sun pops up from a northerly position. Book an upper-story room facing the ocean at the sole hotel. You'll have a great view of the 1,045-foot-long Edwin S. Taylor Folly Beach Fishing Pier and the lively beach.

Above: Hurricane Hugo gave the gift of creativity when it washed this boat ashore. No one ever claimed it, so folks have been painting messages on the boat ever since. You sometimes see people lined up to paint one right after another, each message fading faster than the setting sun. GPS coordinates: 32°41'2" N, 79°57'29" W

Right: The Sand Dollar Social Club has been a Folly Beach stalwart for more than thirty years. Things haven't changed at this private club since—well, never. GPS coordinates: 32°39'18" N, 79°56'25" W

Seabrook Island Beach Club; GPS coordinates: 32°33'35" N, 80°10'21" W

VII. Seabrook Island

www.discoverseabrook.com

Seabrook Island's indigenous population dates back to approximately 200 B.C. The island was first discovered by settlers in 1666, when explorer and future lieutenant governor Robert Sanford planted his flag for England's King Charles. In the late 1800s, the local Stono Indians relinquished the island to the English government, which then sold the property to English settlers.

The island was used as a staging area for Hessian and British troops during the American Revolutionary War. In 1816, it was sold to William Seabrook of nearby Edisto Island, who grew cotton here.

In the early 1900s, Seabrook was sold to sportsmen for hunting, fishing, and recreation, and in 1951, about 1,408 of its acres were given to the Episcopal Diocese of South Carolina.

In 1970, the diocese sold about 1,100 acres to private developers who planned and constructed the private residential community that Seabrook Island is today.

Where: Seabrook Island is on the Atlantic coast, about 24 miles south of Charleston.

Seabrook Equestrian Center is located just after the island entrance gates. The center offers morning rides on the beach, trail rides, pony rides, and lessons. If you bring your horse, they'll board it for you (call ahead to arrange for boarding, 1-866-586-6380). GPS coordinates: 32°35'31" N, 80°9'46" W

Complementary colors are part of the natural order. GPS coordinates: 32°35'15" N, 80°10'54" W

From downtown Charleston, find Bohicket Rd./State Rd. S 10-20, turn left and travel a gorgeous two-lane road through salt marsh, live oaks, and horse farms until you hit the Seabrook, Kiawah roundabout. Seabrook is off to the right.

Noted for: Off the beaten track, Seabrook is home to South Carolina's first fully certified Audubon Cooperative Sanctuary.

Seabrook is an exclusive destination but if you have the coin to spare and the desire to photograph wildlife and plant life in an immaculate setting, it is a great shooter's destination. Its flora and fauna are noteworthy: 2,200 acres of pristine maritime forest replete with majestic oaks, palm trees, live oaks, pines, hickories, magnolias and sweetgum trees. It is also home

to red fox, otters, marsh rabbits, gray squirrels, raccoons, and white-tailed deer. More than 30 species of reptiles and amphibians, including alligators, tree frogs, chameleons, and turtles, can be found on the island.

The Seabrook Island Club has participated in the Audubon North American Birdwatching Open since 1998, often taking top honors. More than 80 species, including federally threatened and endangered birds such as the bald eagle, are routinely spotted on the island. The island's 1,250 human residents are staunch protectors of its ecosystem.

What to Watch for: Unfortunately, Seabrook is private, so much of its beauty is seen only by owners or renters.

You can walk the beach and the nearby marshlands, where brown pelicans, osprey, ibis, and snowy egrets are bound to make an appearance. Skinks, snakes, geckos, alligators, rabbits, and deer are abundant. Sunrise and sunset are the best times to capture animals foraging for food. If you're vigilant, you could see black and gray dolphins throughout the day. The Edisto River region might be the only place in America where dolphins work together in "strand feedings," surrounding a school of fish and driving them to shore. The dolphins then eat up the easy pickings. GPS coordinates: 32°35'7" N, 80°10'22" W

VIII. Edisto Island

www.edistobeach.com

The Edistow Indians were the original inhabitants of this island, until those intrepid settlers the Spanish and the English showed up in the 16th and 17th centuries. Spanish priests arrived to convert the Indians, and Spanish pirates ravaged the region for a while. Otherwise, there's little evidence other than written history to prove the Spanish were ever here.

The English, however, decided to invest, purchasing the island from the Edistows. The settlers developed an agrarian community. Rice was a bust but indigo thrived, and true wealth followed until the Revolutionary War alienated indigo's biggest consumers, the English.

Soon Sea Island cotton arrived, a particularly fine strain that created great wealth for Edistow growers. Many plantations and large homes were built in this era only to fall to ruin with the advent of the Civil War and the abolition of slavery. In the 1920s, the boll weevil turned cotton fields to vegetable patches, and the construction of new homes on the beach brought tourists and new residents. The era of Edisto as a place for vacationers had begun.

Where: Take a left off of US 17 South at the Highway 174 junction and slash through a magnificent, unspoiled landscape steeped in history. Be sure to stop at the Serpentarium, which is truly crawling with reptiles (snake and alligator feedings are a highlight). The Old Post Office Restaurant offers some of the finest dining in the region (it's open for dinner only).

Traverse the McKinley Washington Jr. Bridge. When you have crossed over the Intracoastal Waterway and the Dawhoo River, you've reached Edisto Island. **GPS coordinates: 32°38'48" N, 80°20'34" W**

Edisto is less than an hour from Charleston and Beaufort and roughly two hours from Savannah, Georgia. This 68-square-mile dot of land is located two thirds of the way down the South Carolina coast. There is one hotel/resort and nary a stop light. Any organized entertainment is based in nature. It feels like the middle of nowhere, because, frankly, it is.

Noted for: Nearly half of Edisto is classified as protected, natural land. Your best shooting will be along the beaches, creeks, and marshes. Being near water puts you in the path of animal life. Be sure to bring your tripod; shade from the omnipresent trees means slower shutter speeds.

Since 2008, tourists have been permitted to enter the Botany Bay Plantation Wildlife Management Area. It's a diverse forest and coastal reserve. Its location on the old Botany Bay Plantation makes it a cultural and historical landmark as well. Head to the beach for a sunset swim when you're done shooting.

In 2011, Botany Bay Ecotours will be offering self-guided ecotour apps on its website, www.botanybayplantation.com, that combine cultural and natural history.

Edisto Beach State Park offers a system of biking and hiking trails where you may encounter alligators, wild turkeys, osprey, and white-tailed deer. Bobcats are also known to re-

Bare bones gas station on the Savannah Highway, US 17. Those are my car's headlights lighting the right side of the building. GPS coordinates: 32°45'19" N, 80°20'36" W

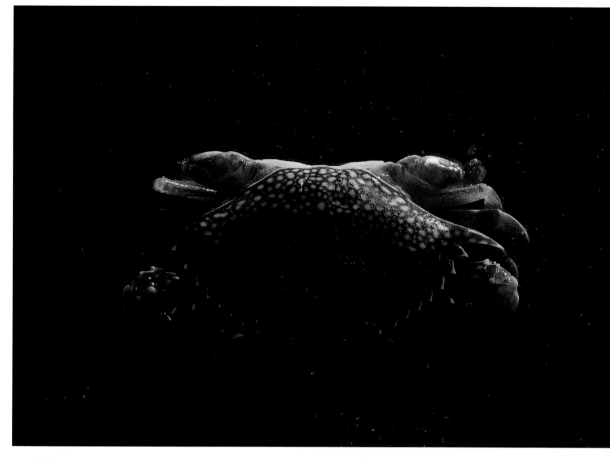

Backlighting and some aggressive vignetting brings out the texture on this crab that was playing opossum.
GPS coordinates: 32°29'57" N, 80°18'7" W

side in this area. Follow the trail along Scott's Creek and visit the second-oldest Native American pottery site in South Carolina, Spanish Mount, a 4,000-year-old oyster shell midden left by the Edistow.

What to Watch for: There are twenty-six historic places listed in the National Registry, and each tells part of Edisto's story.

Self-guided tours will let you set your shooting schedule without the concern of delaying other visitors. There's a 22-mile, overnight, self-guided canoe and kayak trip from Carolina Heritage Outfitters (www.canoesc.com/index

.htm) that includes lodging in a tree house with a sleeping loft. It's situated on a private creek near the river's edge. Clearly, waterproofing your camera is paramount while on the river. Pelican's waterproof camera cases are great, or try The Waterproof Store, www.thewaterproof store.com.

You can find loads of additional eco-tours that will have you paddling or boating next to dolphins, crawling along with loggerhead hatchlings, chasing shrimp, or birding in St. Helena Sound. Ask locals for recommendations.

A little flare from the sunset creeps in at the top of this classic Lowcountry vista. There's not much you can do if you're shooting into a setting sun. Use a small card or your hand to block any light reflecting off your lens. You can see the difference in the viewfinder. You'll lose that white streak across your image and the haze that reduces sharpness. GPS coordinates: 32°35'54" N, 80°20'46" W

Right: A marine Rorschach Test floating in with the tide. GPS coordinates: 32°29'0" N, 80°19'30" W

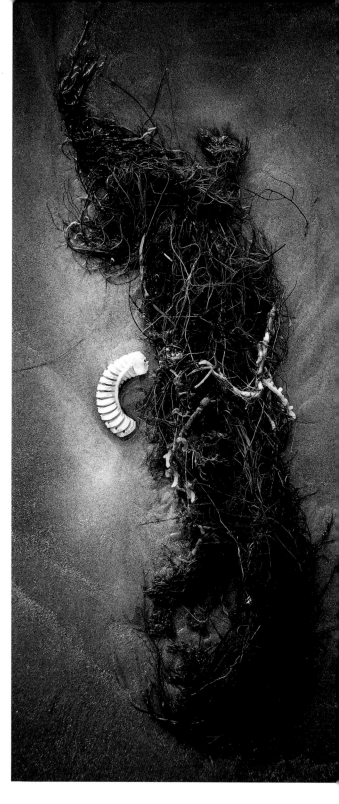

IX. Beaufort

www.cityofbeaufort.org

Beaufort is a charming small city steeped in tradition and folklore. It's easy to negotiate and a delight to explore.

Its history is rich. Native Americans inhabited the region as early as 4000 BC. The largest groups were Cherokee and Catawbas, and their archaeological remnants can be found even today.

Beaufort and Port Royal were discovered by the Spanish in 1514, when the small bay witnessed only the second landing on the North American continent by Europeans. The ever youthful Ponce de Leon had planted his flag in St. Augustine, Florida, only a year earlier.

Despite its early discovery, Beaufort is the state's second-oldest city. Named for Henry Somerset, the second Duke of Beaufort, the town has one of the largest natural harbors on the coast. France and Spain both attempted to settle the region but environment, disease, and Indian attacks sent them packing. Beaufort began to grow as Georgia was settled, providing a buffer zone to Spanish and Indian attacks.

Walking the Old Point neighborhood just east of the downtown commercial area is like wandering through a Thornton Wilder novel. Here, 19th-century antebellum homes are surrounded by white picket fences and live oaks dripping Spanish moss. Walking tours are recommended, and most will include a hike past the Tidalholm Mansion at 1 Laurens Street,

Arrive at a small bridge about 14 miles outside of Jacksonboro. Look to the right and you will find this house on the Ashepoo River. My original composition was much wider, but cropping in on the red roof lent greater impact to the image.
GPS coordinates: 32°44'37" N, 80°33'23" W

Above: One Laurens Street, or the Big Chill *house. Use the lens correction filter in Photoshop or a third-party product such as PTLens to correct lens pincushion, barrel distortion, and perspective in normal and fisheye lenses.* GPS coordinates: 32°26'3" N, 80°39'53" W

Left: Entering Beaufort, Highway 21 becomes Boundary Street. Once past the Beaufort National Cemetery you start to enter the heart of this charming town. Follow Boundary until you can only swing to the right. As you make the final swing into Beaufort on Bellamy Curve, you will see one of the five remaining (of thirty-one total) Beaufort mermaids left from a 2006 arts project sponsored by the Beaufort Arts Council. Miss Beaufort *was decorated by a sister team, one of whom actually held the crown of Miss Beaufort in 1962. I used the camera's built-in flash to fill in a shadowy* Miss Beaufort. GPS coordinates: 32°26'21" N, 80°40'12" W

the home where old friends canoodled in *The Big Chill*.

Beaufort's fortunes seem to rise and fall with the harbor tide. The grand homes along Bay Street were built by 19th-century merchants who blessed Beaufort with the nation's highest per capita income. In the last century the town was beset by fires, storms, and the demise of the phosphate mining industry. Beaufort is a great place to explore, whether your interests are historic or purely visual.

Where: Beaufort can be reached by car from the south via SC 170, and from the north via Highway 21. I-95 feeds both of these roads. You can also travel US 17, Savannah Highway, from Charleston. Most of the trip in either direction is on a single-lane road. Sadly, roadwork is impacting once-quaint spots along the route. For example, the Carolina Cherry Company confection stand was once nestled in the shadow of 80-foot pine trees but it will soon be just another stop on a four-lane thoroughfare.

About 14 miles outside Jacksonboro, on the part of US 17 called the Ace Basin Parkway, you will come to the Ashepoo River. If you're heading into town on Highway 21, watch for the Marine Corps Air Station, with its replicas of old and new fighter planes. I've pulled off the road and shot without interruption from base security or local law enforcement.

If you make an immediate left from Highway

The Carolina Cherry Company on Highway 17 has some great peach and cherry cider combinations. Grab a bag of benne wafers for the ride to Beaufort. I like the cool and warm elements on the edge of this image. GPS coordinates: 32°36'19" N, 80°45'18" W

21 onto Bay Street, you can get a wonderful view of the Richard V. Woods Memorial Bridge and then continue on to the Old Point neighborhood.

The Michael J. Smith Airport in Beaufort is named after the local who commanded the final, unfortunate flight of the Space Shuttle *Challenger*. A small airport serves nearby Lady's Island; it would be the best place to rent a plane for aerial photography. Larger airports can be found in Savannah and Charleston.

Noted for: The Beaufort National Cemetery grounds are resplendent with live oaks and Spanish moss. The cemetery is shaped like a very large semicircle and is divided by roads that emanate from its main gate like the spokes of a wheel. The graves are situated in wedge-shaped sections between the roads. Several Medal of Honor recipients are interred here, as is Colonel Donald Conroy, the Great Santini. The cemetery was listed on the National Register of Historic places in 1997. Bring your tripod—it's densely shaded.

If you continue on Highway 21, over the Woods Memorial Bridge, you can head out to Hunting Island State Park. It's a beautiful setting but I wouldn't recommend camping for

There are four retired fighter planes located at the front entrance of the Marine Corps Air Station on Highway 21. It's about a 15-minute ride from downtown Beaufort. GPS coordinates: 32°27'29" N, 80°44'0" W

Slave quarters at the Penn Center, St. Helena Island GPS coordinates: 32°23'16" N, 80°34'33" W

those looking to shoot. Tents tend to be a security risk and you can bet it will rain when you bring your new Nikon! RV hookups and cabins with full amenities are available.

Day trippers will find plenty to do and to shoot in the park; 4 miles of pristine beach, a classic subtropical forest area with tentacles of hiking trails, a marsh region, and great bird life, as well as alligators, kayaking, and scenic vistas. The beach has a dramatic, eerie, tree graveyard where the surf has killed and knocked down trees near the water's edge.

Head for the marsh boardwalk, which places you smack in the middle of marsh life. The Nature Center fishing pier near the Fripp Island Bridge is the longest freestanding pier on the East Coast. Kayakers, dolphins, sea-

birds, and boaters create a constant string of potential images.

What to Watch for: This area is the home of the Gullah people, descended from West African slaves who were brought to this coast centuries ago to work on the rice plantations. Evidence of their culture is all over greater Beaufort and the islands.

I hear great things about kayak rentals from Barefoot Bubba's, located a mile from Hunting Island State Park. Seeing land from the marsh presents another perspective to Lowcountry life; it also puts you in the neighborhood of dolphins and sea turtles. I never tire of seeing them. Barefoot Bubba's guides are very kind and knowledgeable and they also give away free ice cream. (Yep, free.)

Pass a bit farther down Highway 21 on St. Helena Island and you'll come to Martin Luther King Drive. Grab a bite at Gullah Grub before making a right onto MLK Drive and heading about a mile to a fork in the road. If you swing right, you will quickly come across the St. Helena Parish Chapel ruins. The hollowed-out church is a stellar example of mid-18th-century tabby architecture. Tabby structures were made of a mixture of shells, lime, gravel stone, and water. Tabby was a flexible and inexpensive building material. This area, especially as you head up toward Seaside Road, is traditional Gullah country. Be alert for eyes painted on trees and houses painted bright blue and green to keep the "haints" away. GPS coordinates: 32°22'32" N, 80°34'36" W

Above: Travel a bit farther down MLK Drive and you'll find one of the country's most famous sites for humanitarian endeavors. The Penn School began in 1862 as an experimental program that educated Sea Island slaves who were freed at the beginning of the Civil War. In the 1960s, Dr. Martin Luther King Jr. and the Southern Christian Leadership Conference used the site as a retreat for strategic planning sessions. Today, the Penn Center is a nonprofit organization focused on preserving and promoting Sea Island culture and history. GPS coordinates: 32°23'23" N, 80°34'32" W

Right: Shed detail at the Gay Fish Company docks. Purchase shrimp at their retail store or travel south a bit to the Shrimp Shack. Filmmakers used one of the owner's shrimp boats and dock in the movie Forrest Gump. *GPS coordinates: 32°24'44" N, 80°28'40" W*

Left top: Marsh view from Hunting Island, looking back at St. Helena Island. GPS coordinates: 32°24'42" N, 80°28'38" W

Left bottom: Laundry drop, Seaside Road GPS coordinates: 32°23'44" N, 80°26'28" W

Below: Take Highway 21 South over the Richard V. Woods Memorial Bridge from Beaufort, traverse Lady's Island, and you'll come to St. Helena Island. St. Helena is filled with history, Gullah tradition, and incredible natural beauty. It is not to be missed. This is a colorful window treatment at a food shop off of Highway 21. GPS coordinates: 32°23'48" N, 80°34'40" W

There is no shortage of lighthouses in this coastal region but the Hunting Island Lighthouse is the only lighthouse in South Carolina that is open to the public. Pay your $2 and climb the 167 steps to some of the most expansive views of the coast you'll find anywhere. Completed in 1875, the lighthouse is made of cast iron and brick. It's not functional for navigation but a revolving light turns on at dusk so as not to disappoint the more than a million yearly park visitors. GPS coordinates: 32°22'32" N, 80°26'17" W

X. Bluffton

www.townofbluffton.sc.gov

In 1825, European settlers built a small, breezy hilltop town overlooking the May River. The town of Bluffton soon became a popular refuge from the oppressive inland plantations where yellow fever and malaria ran wild.

Bluffton became a commercial center for plantations and a stop on the ferry route between Savannah and Beaufort. It's said the seeds of secession in South Carolina were sown in Bluffton, taking root in churches and meeting sites such as the Secession Oak (which is still alive but now rests on private property).

Bluffton today is one of the fastest growing towns in South Carolina. The town draws on its reputation as a quirky, artistic, independent community with a notable history.

Where: From I-95 take Highway 278 South to Route 46 (Bluffton Road). Turn right and head to May River Road. Start exploring. The scenic route from Beaufort and Port Royal goes down SC 170 to Highway 278 heading south. Follow the above directions from there.

Noted for: Bluffton has a very cool, quirky artists' community, a perfect complement to its laid-back ambiance. Calhoun Street is a residential and commercial strip that boasts numerous galleries of all kinds. Continue down Calhoun to the May River and the Church of

Head out of Port Royal on Highway 802 West and you will run into the Okatie Highway, Route 170. Pass over the Broad River Bridge, and after 4 miles or so you'll find the Chechesee River. This photo was taken from a small bridge at about 9:30 AM. I boosted the vibrance control on this to give the marsh grass some punch. GPS coordinates: 32°23'39" N, 80°26'25" W

The nearby Caldwell Archive is a large collection of state archives that can be viewed by appointment.

What to Watch for: At 56 Calhoun Street, a bit past Lawrence Street, you will find the Gallery Without Walls, an open-air gallery stocked with art produced on wood and tin procured from derelict tenant homes. www.dpierce giltner.com

The grounds by the Church of the Cross, on the May River, are a lovely spot to spread your red checkerboard tablecloth and picnic away the afternoon.

The Church of the Cross sits near the banks of the May River. I also shot a wider composition to show the river, but this image focuses on the Gothic design and beauty of the structure. Rose-tinted windows bathe the interior with a warm cast. GPS coordinates: 32°13'52" N, 80°51'48" W

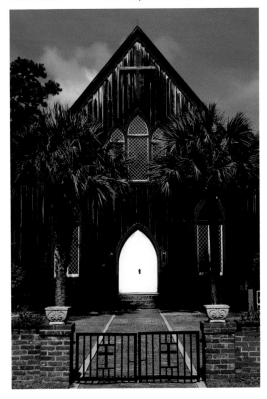

There's lots to do in Bluffton. You won't know which way to turn! GPS coordinates: 32°14'1" N, 80°51'46" W

the Cross. Built by architect E. B. White and consecrated in 1857, it survived the invasion of union troops and was rebuilt after the hurricane of 1898.

The Heyward House was once the residence of a wealthy plantation owner and is now one of just a small handful of antebellum homes remaining in Bluffton, part of its National Register Historic District. Heyward House also serves as Bluffton's unofficial welcome center, where you can grab a walking tour map.

At Gallery Without Walls artist D. Pierce Giltner is delighted to talk about his art, your art, anybody's art. He's a card-carrying character and his enthusiasm is contagious. He loves to capture oystermen and their processes. I burned a ton of photos here. GPS coordinates: 32°14'6" N, 80°51'45" W

Torn flags on the dock at Harbour Town Lighthouse. GPS coordinates: 32°8'19" N, 80°48'48" W

XI. Hilton Head

www.hiltonheadisland.org

After the American Revolution, Hilton Head entered a golden age, suffered during the War of 1812, and returned to glory again until the Civil War. After the war, Hilton Head became a haven for freed slaves. The Gullah people thrived here. Electricity arrived on the island in 1931 and it's hard to believe residents received their first telephone as recently as 1960.

Hilton Head today is a labyrinth of residential and commercial areas surrounded by stunning Lowcountry geography and deep cultural history. Many of the residential subdivisions were developed around original plantation boundaries.

Where: Two airports service Hilton Head; tiny Hilton Head Airport is on the island and Savannah/Hilton Head International Airport is 45 miles south. If you're riding in from Beaufort and Port Royal on SC 170, grab Highway 278 for a shorter trip.

Noted for: It's difficult to believe so many resorts could be packed onto a 12-mile-long, 5-mile-wide island. But you never sense crowding because they're all tucked behind gates and walls of trees. Hilton Head has done a great job of zoning commercial complexes to preserve the natural beauty.

Hilton Head is home to four nature preserves: Sea Pines Forest Preserve, Newhall Audubon Preserve, Fish Haul Park, and Pinckney Island Preserve.

Newhall is great for bird watching. It's located on the south end of the island and offers 50 acres of pristine forest, guided tours, paths to walk, and tagged plant life.

Pinckney Island Preserve is right in the middle of the Intracoastal Waterway. Explore 4,000

At Lake Joe, Sea Pines Preserve; GPS coordinates: 32°8'26" N, 80°46'36" W

acres of salt marsh and maritime habitat while biking or walking its 14 miles of pathways.

I hit the trail at Sea Pines Preserve, a series of wetlands and ridges formed by changing sea levels over the past 15,000 years. Tripod and camera on my shoulder, I entered through the Greenwood Entrance and chose a two-hour walk amidst horseback riders, baby alligators, and a wealth of bird and insect life. The Indian Shell Ring Trail shoots off from here. It's a short hike to the shell ring, which is simply a plot of land with a sign recognizing the location. There are no shells, only trees and grass to shoot.

Located just off Highway 278, Zion Cemetery is all that remains of the Zion Chapel of Ease, a small church built for plantation owners. Interred in the cemetery are soldiers who fought in the Revolutionary War. The Baynard Mausoleum is the oldest intact structure on Hilton Head Island. **GPS coordinates: 32°12'5" N, 80°41'58" W**

Kayaks lined up on the beach, ready for a class. My 200mm zoom was maxed out with a wide-open aperture. Here is where you really need to understand the exposure variables of your camera—I'd wanted to isolate the word, "perception" in this shot. If I had shot this at f16, too many of the boats would have been in focus for the photograph to be at all effective. GPS coordinates: 32°8'19" N, 80°48'48" W

Bring a tripod as much of the walk is covered by a dense canopy. A macro lens for close-up work is recommended as well. I was not carrying a macro lens when I was there, and I missed shooting some insects and flowers I'd have liked to get.

Your camera's built-in flash is great for fill-in work in this type of setting. I use it more than I ever imagined I would. In addition, be ready to use your lens's manual focus. Many times I found myself in spots that were too dark or had very little contrast. Your autofocus lens

Daufuskie Island is a 1-hour, $45-round-trip ferry ride from Hilton Head. Try Calibogue Cruises from the Broad Creek Marina. Daufuskie is Gullah, meaning "the first key" or "the first island." Daufuskie is home to the largest Gullah population in the United States. Yes, there are alligators as well as a bounty of Lowcountry wildlife to photograph. GPS coordinates: 32°5'53" N, 80°53'53" W

wants to see some definition between a light and dark area in the scene and won't fire when there is none. In tough focusing situations, if your camera allows, use the live view option on the LCD screen. Compose the image and then use the zoom function to get a close-up view of whatever you're focusing on. This procedure is not practical if you're shooting quickly but works well with the tripod for landscapes and interiors.

What to Watch for: The Windmill Harbor area has all sorts of activities happening just offshore. Bring a long lens to photograph jet skiers, parasailers, water skiers and kayakers.

For good people photography, consider attending some of the numerous festivals that occur annually. There's the Seafood, Brew & Jazz Festival, the Italian Heritage Festival, the Hilton Head Oyster Festival, and Bark in the Park. The Annual Master Gardener Garden Tour allows you access to private homes and gardens.

Of particular interest is the Gullah Heritage Trail Tour (www.gullaheritage.com/tour.html). Remarkably, Gullah culture and traditions have survived since before the Civil War. Tour through ten family-based compounds, a one-room schoolhouse, and plantation tabby ruins.

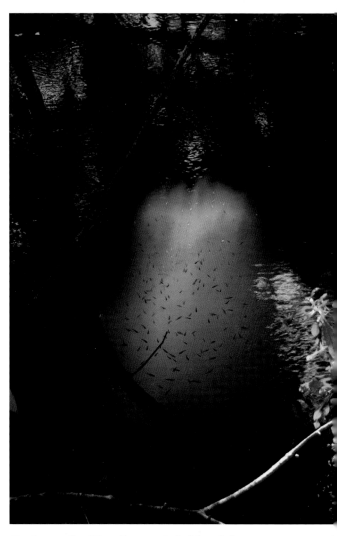

During my Sea Pines Preserve trek, I found that the water coming from a pipe was attracting small fish. I wanted to preserve image quality and shoot at a low ISO. The water surrounding the fish was absolutely dark, so to get any detail I had to increase my exposure, though I was already shooting wide open. If I slowed down the shutter speed too much the moving fish would be too blurry. I had no choice but to increase the ISO and reduce noise in software. GPS coordinates: 32°8'45" N, 80°46'51" W

Window at the Corner of Bull Street and West Charlton. GPS coordinates: 32°4'16" N, 81°5'43" W

XII. Savannah

www.savannahga.gov

Founded in 1733 by Englishman James Oglethorpe and 114 men, women, and children, Savannah began as a haven for English debtors and religious devotees (except Catholics).

Savannah's founders intended to create a trade and commercial center and to act as a protective buffer between northern colonies and the Spanish in Florida. Only three formal laws ruled the city: no hard liquor, no slaves, and no lawyers.

Savannah was America's first planned city. James Oglethorpe's design called for the creation of open squares for meeting spaces and public service.

In 1793 Eli Whitney invented the cotton gin here. Cotton became Savannah's major export and fueled the construction of many area masterpieces. Regrettably, two epic fires that swept the city mean little remains from this period.

After the Civil War, cotton kept the city vital until nationwide production lowered prices and the boll weevil arrived.

After the Great Depression, grand homes and boulevards fell into disrepair. The city seemed bent on paving over the past until the Historic Savannah Foundation established a revolving fund in the 1950s to save homes from demolition.

Savannah's original designs remain today, with more than twenty squares anchoring an orderly grid of beautiful streets and buildings. The squares have been designated as National Historic Civil Engineering Landmarks and a 2.2-square-mile downtown area containing thousands of architecturally important buildings was named a Historic Landmark District.

Sweetgrass gatherers are not easy to spot. I swung my tripod around to grab this shot. GPS coordinates: 32°4'56" N, 81°5'34" W

Savannah is a photographer's urban dream and a fun place to spend some time. It's quite manageable, easy to negotiate, and teeming with young, interesting people. I photographed a straight path from the river to Forsyth Park and it took the entire day.

Do your research, plan a route, and then add a day to your visit. A tripod is de rigueur for architectural work. There's good people shooting along River Street, the revitalized warehouse district. On East River Street you can sample some of the microbreweries, hop a riverboat, or book a ghost walk.

Savannah is for shooters.

Where: Fly into the Savannah/Hilton Head International Airport, just 8 miles outside of town. Take I-95 south from the airport to Route 16 east, and that will bring you to the downtown area.

Noted for: Where to begin? Savannah's port is a beehive of container ships loading and unloading. Huge ships passing on the Savannah River dwarf the River Street promenade. It's one of the ten busiest seaports in the United States.

Savannah holds two National Historic Landmark districts, several National Register entries, and multiple local landmarks, presenting a deep inventory of architectural subjects to photograph.

Architectural styles range from Victorian to Gothic Revival. The city is a model for heritage conservation worldwide. On the north side, the Victorian District grew as a response to overcrowding in the Historic District. It was considered Savannah's first suburb, composed of stately brick mansions and small cottages.

Sometimes it's the content and not the container that's of interest. You may, for example, want to visit the birthplace of Girl Scouts founder Juliette Gordon Low.

Or you may care to record the locations of the various movies shot in Savannah, includ-

Relax and play the plantation owner for an hour in your rented horse and carriage. It's a great way to marinate in Savannah's historic ambiance. Think shutter speed when moving and bumping your way along. **GPS coordinates: 32°4'51" N, 81°5'40" W**

The array of food and shopping venues on Riverwalk is dazzling. Again, a long lens compresses the scene. GPS coordinates: 32°4'53" N, 81°5'26" W

ing *Forrest Gump, Midnight in the Garden of Good and Evil, Bagger Vance, Roots, Glory,* and *The General's Daughter.* If you're going to photograph Paula Deen's Lady and Sons Restaurant, get there when morning light hits the front of the building.

What to Watch for: You may want to coordinate your visit with the raucous St. Patrick's Day Parade and celebrations. Mingle with 750,000 of your newest friends and grab a hard disk full of fun images. You might even consider a waterproof housing for this shoot.

The March Savannah Music Festival may enhance your performance portfolio. Check out the Jazz Festival in late September for a selection of local and national talent.

Great shooting opportunities abound at the Savannah Asian Festival in June. In addition to the requisite food stalls there are cultural exhi-

bitions as well as workshops such as Indian henna tattoo art, Chinese calligraphy, and Filipino pole dance.

In late November, Savannah kicks off the holiday season with a festive display of more than 60 decked-out boats cruising the Savannah River. Bring a tripod and remote release for the evening fireworks display. Use a low ISO setting and experiment with the first couple of bursts. Fireworks are pretty bright and they will light up quite a bit of the surroundings.

One trick is to set your shutter speed to "bulb" (always open). Get a black card and start your exposure with it placed in front of your lens. Every time you see a burst, pull the card away from the lens and you will capture multiple bursts on one image. Release the shutter to proceed to the next frame. In addition, focus and lock it down before dark. It's much easier than constantly trying to focus at night.

Above: Vignette of the Forsyth Park fountain. The park's design was supposedly influenced by the urban renewal taking place in Paris in the 1850s. Large boulevards and parks were all the rage and the Forsyth is thought to be a copy of the fountain in Place de la Concorde in Paris. When photographing water or glass, always try to light it from behind to enhance detail. GPS coordinates: 32°4'13" N, 81°5'42" W

Right: A tug nudges a departing container ship. A long focal length lens will draw two subjects closer and create more drama. GPS coordinates: 32°4'54" N, 81°5'27" W

Above: A bronze statue of Oscar-winning lyricist Johnny Mercer stands near Ellis Square. I used my camera's flash to generate detail in the part of the statue that was in shadow; GPS coordinates: 32°4'50" N, 81°5'39" W

Left: A statue of Raphael seems to contemplate the current show at the Telfair Museum, the oldest public art museum in the South (http://telfair .org). The Telfair was designed in the Regency style by English architect William Jay. Open up your lens and adjust your shutter speed if you want to blur the background and focus attention on the statue. GPS coordinates: 32°4'43" N, 81°5'42" W

Bicyclist in Daffin Park and a good example of the benefits of backlighting water. GPS coordinates: 32°2'51" N, 81°5'4" W

The African American Families Monument on River Street behind City Hall; GPS coordinates: 32°4'54" N, 81°5'27" W

A quiet moment at the band shell in Daffin Park. It's off Route 80, on the way to Tybee Island. GPS coordinates: 32°2'45" N, 81°5'2" W

XIII. Tybee Island

www.tybeeisland.com

The Spanish were once again first on the scene at Tybee, but superior settlements installed by the French and British upriver at Savannah shook loose Spain's grip. The French wanted Tybee for the sassafras root they believed to be a miracle cure.

Savannah's founder, James Oglethorpe, knew that the port city of Savannah could not survive without a secured landfall at the mouth of the Savannah River. Tybee Island, the largest and outermost strip of land, was outfitted with a small fort and the first of four lighthouses that would adorn the island.

Tybee played important roles in many of South Carolina's conflicts. It was the staging area for Colonial troops before the ill-fated siege of Savannah. During the War of 1812, Tybee's lighthouse beacon was used to warn Savannah of impending British attack. Its use as a test ground for the Union's new rifled cannon resulted in the devastation of Confederate troops at Fort Pulaski and rendered all similar forts obsolete. In 1855, Fort Screven was built here, serving an integral role in America's coastal defense system until 1947.

Since the Civil War, Tybee has been a retreat for Savannans escaping the city heat. Only 15 miles from Savannah, its quirky, friendly, and eclectic population prohibits any pretense. It's a great place to go for a weekend of shooting open-air galleries, abundant avian life, and scenery and wildlife on the salt marsh trails.

Fort Pulaski (Cockspur Island) taken from the north (back) side. A young lieutenant just out of West Point, Robert E. Lee, oversaw the construction of the dikes and drainage system. GPS coordinates: 32°1'42" N, 80°53'28" W

Cockspur Lighthouse seen from the end of the Lighthouse Overlook Trail. GPS coordinates: 32°1'21" N, 80°53'1" W

Where: From downtown Savannah find East Victory Drive (43rd Street) heading east. This turns into Route 80, which will take you directly to Tybee Island. This is the only route in or out, unless you're on a boat.

Noted for: In 1862 the top portion of Tybee's lighthouse was set ablaze by Confederate troops so the Union could not use it to guide their ships into port. The bottom 60 feet of the lighthouse dates from 1773 and the top 94 feet were added in 1867. It is the oldest and tallest lighthouse in Georgia.

Tybee is a barrier island and part of the Colonial Coast Birding Trail. Its salt marshes contain scores of egrets, herons, and ibises, and you might even see an endangered wood stork. North Beach near the lighthouse is the best spot in winter and fall to spot migrating shore-birds. The mouth of the Savannah River is the winter home to loons, ruddy ducks, and mergansers. This north beach area is great for shelling, panning for fossil sharks' teeth, and dolphin gazing.

The best way to see and shoot this region is by boat. If you rent a boat or charter a tour service, be sure to visit Little Tybee Island. There are absolutely no amenities but you can tour or camp there. Bald eagles and osprey nest on the island.

The Tybee Island Marine and Science Center offers adult classes, outings, and camps for children. It's located in the central downtown area.

Find the turnoff of Route 80 and take a quick trip across the marsh to the Fort Pulaski Monument. You'll see signs just before reaching Tybee. Remnants of Union shelling can be seen in the sides of the structure. Take a trail out to the Cockspur Lighthouse and you may spy a painted bunting. It is the official bird of Tybee Island.

What to Watch for: Sign up for the annual 5K Turtle Trot to benefit the Tybee Island Sea Turtle Project. After the 2010 race, the Georgia Sea Turtle Center released a rehabilitated loggerhead back into the ocean. Racers are on their marks the third week of April.

Don't miss the Sally Pearce Nature Trail off of Highway 80 and 5th Avenue. This native maritime forest hosts loads of birds, including thirty species of warblers every spring.

Tybee's Seafood and Music Festival in April combines a carnival atmosphere (including rides) with live musical entertainment and memorable local seafood. It's a two-day event that should keep you busy.

In June it's time for the annual Tybee Tour of Homes. Amble through old and new structures and you may come away with an architectural portfolio piece or two.

Be careful not to get caught up in the annual Beach Bum Parade in May. This is a water-throwing, water-gun-shooting free-for-all that will have you grabbing for your waterproof camera housing. Some shooters will want to stake out a two-story-high vantage point for this event!

View from the bridge that crosses Turners Creek from Whitemarsh Island to Wilmington Island, on the way to Tybee. GPS coordinates: 32°2'6" N, 80°59'12" W

Above: Shrubs and shadows, Lighthouse Overlook Trail; GPS coordinates: 32°1'51" N, 80°53'4" W

Left: Fruit of the palmetto palm photographed on the Lighthouse Overlook Trail at Fort Pulaski. The trail guides visitors along open marsh as well as forest, offering views of the Savannah River and Tybee Island. The ¾-mile trail also offers the best views of the historic Cockspur Island Lighthouse. GPS coordinates: 32°1'33" N, 80°53'5" W

Egrets near the old Tybee rail line that once connected Savannah to the Tybee Island beaches. GPS coordinates: 32°2'24" N, 80°56'40" W

Tybee Island Lighthouse; GPS coordinates: 32°1'21" N, 80°50'45" W